D0076450

BASICS
FASHION MANAGEMENT

VISUAL MERCHANDISING FOR FASHION

Sarah Bailey and Jonathan Baker

Fairchild Books
An imprint of Bloomsbury Publishing Plc

BLOOMSBURY
LONDON · NEW DELHI · NEW YORK · SYDNEY

Fairchild Books
An imprint of Bloomsbury Publishing Plc

50 Bedford Square
London
WC1B 3DP
UK

1385 Broadway
New York
NY 10018
USA

www.bloomsbury.com

FAIRCHILD BOOKS, BLOOMSBURY and the Diana logo are
trademarks of Bloomsbury Publishing Plc

First published in 2014
Reprinted 2015

© Bloomsbury Publishing Plc 2014

Sarah Bailey and Jonathan Baker have asserted their rights under the Copyright,
Designs and Patents Act, 1988, to be identified as author of this work.

All rights reserved. No part of this publication may be reproduced or transmitted in
any form or by any means, electronic or mechanical, including photocopying,
recording, or any information storage or retrieval system, without prior permission in
writing from the publishers.

No responsibility for loss caused to any individual or organization acting on or
refraining from action as a result of the material in this publication can be accepted
by Bloomsbury or the author.

British Library Cataloguing-in-Publication Data
A catalogue record for this book is available from the British Library.

ISBN: PB: 978-2-940496-12-9
    ePDF: 978-2-940447-70-1

Library of Congress Cataloging-in-Publication Data
Bailey, Sarah, 1976- author.
Visual merchandising for fashion/Sarah Bailey and Jonathan Baker.
p. cm.
Includes bibliographical references and index.
ISBN 978-2-940496-12-9 (alk. paper) – ISBN 978-2-940447-70-1 (alk.
paper) 1. Fashion merchandising. 2. Display of merchandise. I. Baker, Jonathan,
1967- author. II. Title.
HF6161.C44B35 2013
746.9'20688-dc23
2013020873

Design Pony Ltd.
www.ponybox.co.uk
Printed and bound in China

Ralph Pucci mannequin collection
by Cofrad.

TABLE OF CONTENTS

INTRODUCTION

Visual merchandising puts the art and design back into retail. It plays an important creative and commercial role in many fields including fashion, interiors, film, television, events and exhibitions. It is essential for anyone working in the retail industry to fully engage with the principal stages of design research and realisation in order to strengthen a visual retail brand proposition in the market place. Visual merchandising is often underestimated and overlooked by many retailers, yet is a vital part of the retail business and adds enormous value.

This book presents various visual merchandising techniques and solutions through examples of research, exploration, interpretation, construction and installation. It will discuss concept development from two-dimensional drawings to three-dimensional computer-aided design, as well as the physical elements of creating successful interior retail display design.

The creative and strategic journey within the business of fashion visual merchandising begins by exploring in depth one of the most potent areas of design – communication. This involves making cultural site visits on an international scale, examining window and interior displays and all of the other components that make up visual merchandising through art, architecture, design and natural forms, and recording these visits through sketches and photographs and producing them three dimensionally through the use of different materials. Further investigation into mark making and working in three dimensions is an important form of visual language and communication.

The sense of journey from private spaces to public places is held in fascination. Where do people meet before they go shopping? Why do we go to a particular store and not another? What makes things sell? What first attracts us to a brand? There is a certain level of human psychology that influences the consumer's decision making, which we aim to explore further by case studies.

The aim of this book is to help visual merchandisers develop new ways of working within the fashion retail business. Examples are used to highlight and amplify the theoretical narratives existing in consumer spaces. The complexities of retail spatial design, manipulation of shopper orientation and assessment of space hierarchy contribute to the overall visual merchandising strategy; but of paramount importance is the attraction and enticement of customers by creating the ultimate visual retail experience. How do we define these spaces to maintain commerciality and create an 'experience' to encapsulate the virtual world as well as the physical one?

Visual Merchandising for Fashion aims to provide you with the fundamental skills and knowledge to inspire your conceptual thinking and commercial practice within the competitive visual retail environment.

1

THE CUSTOMER EXPERIENCE

1

What is visual merchandising? Why do we do it and how far does it reach across the fashion industries? Designing the customer shopping experience has never been so important to fashion retailers in order to increase brand awareness and loyalty and to connect with the consumer on a deeper level. In an ever-evolving landscape of omni-channel retailing, the physical shopping experience is emphasised as being one of the most important platforms to visually market products. This chapter aims to explore visual merchandising as entertainment, a live brand experience, a commercial and visual communication tool as well as a marketing opportunity.

1   The design of Topshop's White City store reflects the brand's dedication to youthful, affordable fashion.

What is visual merchandising?

The business of visual merchandising should be viewed as a process from concept to completion, with the purpose of clearly identifying a brand, maintaining brand values, enticing the customer into a commercial space, and keeping them there as long as possible. Visual merchandising is the crucial link between brand, consumer, product and environment; it should entice the customer into the commercial space, engage them and encourage them to spend money.

Why do we do it?

× To communicate the brand identity
× To increase the profile of the brand
× To add visual excitement and impact
× To create atmosphere
× To display product / service width
× To provide advertising opportunities
× To increase sales
× To attract and draw customers into the store
× To maximise space and product effectively
× To simplify the shopping experience

Designing for the fashion brand

The starting point for any visual merchandising scheme is the product and brand. The brand itself acts as the main factor for any direction or execution. This remains true for visual merchandising for fashion. If your brand is a luxury one – tailored and exclusive, for example – the visual merchandising scheme will need to reflect these product and brand values in order to reach its target customers.

It is equally important to consider the type of product along with its features and benefits: how is the product bought and what is it used for?

The visual merchandiser's role is to create the point of visual differentiation for any brand. For example, numerous retailers sell white shirts, but how can one white shirt be represented differently from another shirt by another brand? The challenges lie with the visual merchandiser to create something totally enticing to the consumer. By examining the brand identity and values we can make several 'connections' with the audience. The brand identity can be made up of:

× Brand ethos
× Product type
× Appeal to consumer
× Features and benefits
× Type or level of service

2 RRL NEW YORK MUSIC LIFESTLE

Window installations from Ralph Lauren's RRL store, New York. While much of the lateral thinking behind the overall visual merchandising concept is derived from the product and brand itself, more conceptual designs can be created around customer lifestyles, social statements and trends. This is explored in more detail in chapter 3.

◀ What is visual merchandising?   Where do visual merchandisers work? ▶

12

Designing the customer experience

As we have seen, visual merchandising is all about selling the product and brand to the customer. Creating a connection with the audience triggers an emotive response, which will encourage them to buy into that brand. The visual merchandiser can create this experience for the customer in a number of ways: window installations can be designed to attract, shock, entertain and seduce its viewers; store layouts can be used to guide customers past particular products and visual effects can be used to draw the eye to a particular display. All of these techniques are examined further in chapter 4.

Visual merchandising elements

By assessing the physical space opportunities within the store, such as the floor, ceiling and wall treatments, we are able to understand the constituent elements of visual merchandising:

Macro overview (large scale overview)

- Space layout – how the product positioning reflects the brand (such as luxury minimal or value stacked in volume, for example)
- Live brand experience - visual identity, style and representation
- Store guide - navigation, signposting and direction leading to product or services
- Communication tool - narrative, storytelling and signature of brand through visual merchandising
- Commercial tool - silent selling, price points and merchandising to increase sales
- Marketing opportunity - promotional collateral, supporting wider external marketing campaign
- Entertainment - engage consumer in other aspects of the store, escapism and inspiration
- Art/creative - conceptual art , unique selling point and point of difference from other stores

12. Installation and rollout

11. Cost and budget scheme, quantity and allocation management

1. Retailer or client to brief project, timeframe, and budget

10. Prototype designs for approval

2. Examine the product, brand and environment

9. Source materials, props, display suppliers

VISUAL MERCHANDISING SCHEME LIFECYCLE

3. Research ideas and themes

8. Visually present 2D and 3D designs to client to approve

4. Sketch 2D idea and visually present research

7. Translate design illustrations into 3D CAD or Model

5. Review and discuss ideas and client requirements

6. Research one idea further in more depth using mood boards, sample boards, colour boards etc.

3

Micro overview (small scale, what factors make up the retail space)

- × High level – ceiling, walls, lighting, architecture, graphics, overhead signage, display product
- × Eye level – product positioning, mannequins, props, point of sale, main focal points, countertop installations, graphics
- × Ground level – fixtures, seating, layouts, densities, product positioning, flooring, lighting, pathways, floor graphics
- × Windows – including fascia, store front and entrance
- × Service areas – seating rest areas, circulation paths, cash-taking facilities, changing room facilities, customer service areas such as personal shopping, tailoring and body scanning.

The creative lifecycle of visual merchandising schemes

The creative lifecycle of generating and implementing visual merchandising schemes generally works around supplier lead times, delivery dates, trading and marketing calendars. Sourcing props and materials can sometimes dictate the amount of time available to deliver an entire visual scheme. So, the more complicated the scheme with numerous suppliers for example, the more complex the organisation and coordination of the actual launch.

On average, a window scheme is changed every 5–8 weeks in a large retail business, with smaller product and micro changes (within the same theme) occurring every 1–2 weeks.

Smaller independent retailers tend to change their windows more frequently; installations can be more individual and bespoke for the target audience. This type of operation has much more flexibility but often fewer resources than a larger company set up, so the need to be more creative with a lower budget is paramount.

3 LIFECYCLE OF A VISUAL MERCHANDISING SCHEME

This diagram shows 12 key steps in the production of a display scheme.

Where do visual merchandisers work?

With the growing global marketplace and the constant evolution of digital selling environments, the traditional role of the visual merchandiser no longer applies. The role covers a broad spectrum and a wide range of skills. Here, we will focus on roles within the fashion industry.

The visual merchandising studio

Historically located in the basement or the eaves of the retail space, the visual merchandising studio is where all creative ideas are developed. A specific space allocated for storage and preparation of visual merchandising props, graphics, materials and merchandise is very important, enabling scheme changes to appear seamless to customers. Depending on how the team is split, there could be areas for graphic designers, illustrators or brand creatives to work and more creative, physical areas for visual merchandisers to experiment. As the roles within visual merchandising diversify, it is important that the working environment is designed to reflect the activity. Space is usually at a premium within retail, which poses instant challenges as to how the working space should be organised into selling space, storage or communication/working areas.

4 GANT RUGGER
SHOWROOM

Showroom for Gant Rugger store.

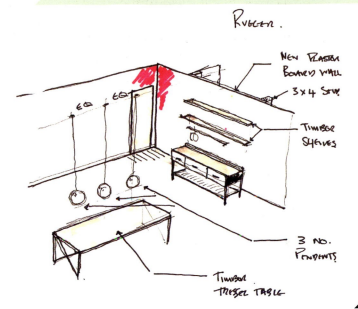

The mock store and window space

For most large retailers, an intentional space for visual merchandisers to practise new techniques and to trial and implement new schemes is paramount to the business. It is important to test new concepts and to assess that a scheme or a physical prototype works, before it is rolled out to multiple stores at a heavy financial cost. In practice, fashion companies tend to select an existing trading store; it could be a store that needs renovation or uplift visually, or a flagship store where high-level visual concepts are derived and watered down for mass rollout. Some fashion companies have a physical 'mock shop' space; this is essentially an augmented store not open to the public, which is used for experimentation, to test visual ideas and products on the shelf, and to photograph and present products to potential buyers.

The showroom

The showroom is similar to a high-street store, but the space is only accessible to buyers, merchandisers, allocators, designers and head office retail staff. Its primary function is to act as a selling space for new products to external buyers, franchises, concessions or department stores.

Visual merchandising roles

Visual merchandising isn't always based in-store. Some other roles include:
× Visual merchandising stylist
× Visual merchandising for magazines
× Visual merchandising journalist
× Mannequin designer
× Prop supplier
× Visual merchandiser for events
× Visual merchandise photographer
× Visual merchandise blogger
× Online visual merchandiser
× Visual merchandising trainer
× Visual merchandising illustrator
× Visual merchandising communications

◀ Where do visual merchandisers work?   Interview: Maxine Groucutt, Liberty, London, UK ▶

16

Working in the visual merchandising industry

Visual merchandising can be a competitive industry to break into so it's a good idea to prepare as best you can. Studying the subject at university is an excellent springboard into industry and offers opportunities to gain a better understanding of the business, enter competitions, test and try new ideas, develop intellectual as well as practical skills and to build up a portfolio of work. Being in education also affords the time to build up a series of networks within industry, which is particularly important.

Work experience is also essential, enabling you to build on your skills, networking opportunities and to develop your portfolio of work. There is no simple way of entering this very desirable profession, apart from determination and perseverance. The starting point could be to gain experience with another visual merchandiser, a supplier to the retail industry, a retail establishment or magazine, or simply offer your visual merchandising services to friends and colleagues for free.

However you gain experience, it is always wise to ensure that you keep a photographic or other visual record of your work to build up your portfolio. Create a resource book or research file: gather as much product information as you can, such as catalogues of props, mannequins and samples of materials; this also helps to communicate your level of understanding of the visual merchandising industry. Keep any inspirational visual reference, such as scrap books of interesting magazine articles, and create a library of visual merchandising and general design books that cover creative processes and historical information.

Verbal and visual presentation skills are critical in visual merchandising and, although not all clients require concepts to be presented on boards, they may expect it digitally. To be able to communicate visual ideas simply and effectively, to people who may not understand a creative process, is an essential skill.

Roles in visual merchandising vary from creative visual artistic director through to the more analytical space planning or visual communication jobs. Depending on your own personal strengths and weaknesses you can assess the kind of job in the industry that would be right for you.

As with any business, employers in visual merchandising have their own requirements and preferences for the type of applicants that they are looking for. The list below covers the main areas for visual merchandising:

× Reliability and punctuality
× Creativity
× Practical skills
× Computer skills
× Team-working skills
× Ability to work effectively alone, taking your own initiative
× Problem-solving skills
× Communication skills
× Willingness to learn, enthusiasm and passion for the subject
× Inspiring and motivating others in the business
× Effective time-management skills
× Subject specific awareness
× Company knowledge

Positive aspects

Artistic – the role is mainly creative and inspiring, always generating new ideas and sourcing concepts.

Practical – many of the roles in visual merchandising require practical work and involve working in different sites every day, working with different people.

Exposure – the opportunity to show your work to a wide audience.

Team work – centred on working together as part of a team of visual merchandisers.

Variety – work can differ from one day to the next as with the nature of changing schemes.

Travel – opportunities to work abroad for a particular brand and international stores.

Negative aspects

Working hours – visual merchandisers sometimes work through the night installing concepts and schemes to avoid disruption during trading hours.

Physical – the job requires much personal stamina and coordination.

Justification – just because something looks good doesn't mean it will sell, visual teams are often challenged by sales managers over performance targets and commercial decisions. Communicating visual merchandising to non-creatives can be tricky.

Interpretation – communicating to suppliers and colleagues about the interpretation of schemes can be challenging. Rolling out display schemes to international stores; fashion trends and styling can be easily mis-interpreted in different environments.

Competitive – this is an artistic retail role that is highly competitive, as with many arts-based jobs.

Portfolio

Your portfolio is your 'ace card' and the best way for a potential employer to assess your current level of skill. If you are called for an interview, you will have to demonstrate some of these skills and therefore it is critical that the work you show is your own. We are often asked what a portfolio should contain and we always recommend the following:

× Only show examples of what you can do well, rather than areas that need further development. An interviewer will want to know what you can contribute to their company rather than what they will need to spend on your development to match the skills of other employees.

× Tailor and edit your portfolio so that its main focus is the company interviewing you: it should be geared to the job role or meets the job skills as advertised.

× Only show the last few examples of projects completed, which should be your best pieces.

× Visual merchandising is about presentation, so ensure that any work shown to a potential employer is beautifully and professionally produced.

× Online portfolios are a good way to communicate your work before and after any meeting.

Interview: Maxine Groucutt, Liberty, London, UK

Maxine Groucutt studied fashion and costume design. She has worked for Warehouse, Miss Selfridge and Polo Ralph Lauren. She is now Head of Visual Identity at Liberty London.

Q **What is your background and how to you get to this point in your career?**

A Originally, I studied fashion and costume design at college. I gravitated towards retail, working up to management level and approached one of our visual merchandisers or 'display' as it was then called, to enquire about how to enter the profession. At this time, I was working at the fashion brand Warehouse. I later became the visual coordinator at Miss Selfridge.

My personal career path has been a very gradual one working with a whole variety of high street and luxury brands through the visual merchandising and management ranks to where I am now, as head of visual identity for a luxury brand.

Q **Who is in your team and what are their back grounds?**

A We have a team of 12: one assistant looking after windows and one who looks after interiors and then a team of visual merchandisers, two managers and four people who look after graphics. All of my team are creative and their backgrounds range from a jewellery designer, a former vet, to a fine artist or they have been promoted from the sales floor.

Oddly I have never interviewed anyone from a purely VM background, they just do not seem to apply for the positions so most of the team is composed of people who dropped into the visual merchandising industry. Having a strong team that really understands the Liberty brand enables us to achieve much better value for money.

Q **What does your role involve?**

A My current role involves looking after everything visual at Liberty. This includes designing the window schemes in conjunction with my team, in-store visual merchandising, interior architecture, and in-store and external graphics and communication. As a team we work from concept design to completion on everything we do. I initially come up with the overall look and feel of a new concept for the first half of the year and communicate where I see the direction going creatively, then the team and I discuss the concepts we are going to implement, which I then develop further, so it is quite an organic process.

Interview: Maxine Groucutt, Liberty, London, UK

Q **Where do you think the visual proposition at Liberty is pitched in terms of its visual merchandising?**

A I would say that at Liberty we focus on collaborations and in particular craftsmanship, so our unique selling point is about the 'curated object'. Historically the brand from its beginning in 1875 began with selling objets d'art and promoted craftsmanship from such places as Japan, the Middle East and Asia. Arthur Lasenby Liberty was the original collaborator working with William Morris and Gabriel Dante Rossetti.

Today we collaborate with artists/designers and brands like Manolo Blahnik, Hermès and Grayson Perry. So, from its origins Liberty curated products from around the world and offered craftsmanship at competitive prices and we maintain these values today with our passion for art, design and craftsmanship. Through our visual merchandising proposition we consider everything about design within our fashion rooms; I always keep in mind how creatively we can add value to the product.

Q **What is the process from concept to completion of your visual merchandising and how long does it take to develop a concept?**

A We tend to work three months in advance when developing new schemes so we are always ahead in our planning. It takes a couple of weeks to work through a concept with initial meetings, finding samples and discussing all the different elements to reach the 'sign off' stage. We also produce mood boards of the overall scheme, with each individual window scheme roughly sketched with a colour chart and map out where the various elements are going to sit. Also, when we work on collaborations we begin with an initial concept and decide what form the collaboration will be and what it may consist of. The collaboration we worked on with Manolo Blahnik was produced to be site specific for the Liberty store whereas our collaboration with Dr Martens was part of a larger, worldwide rollout. Therefore, there are two very different strategies that we need to work through for the business and consider mutual benefits for Liberty and the associated brand.

Q Is sustainability an important consideration within your design? What happens to an old scheme once it is changed?

A When we design a visual merchandising scheme we have to consider how the scheme translates from the windows to the store environment. All objects we use, such as props that we source at markets and fairs, have at least nine lives and we keep reinventing and reworking them. For example, we change the colours, the textures or cover something in a new material; therefore everything has a certain amount of longevity.

Q Is the use of technology an important part of the commercial environment at Liberty?

A Technology is certainly going to be a huge part of retailing in the future and at the moment we are assessing the best use of visual technology for us as a brand. How we are going to use technology is particularly critical as it has to have a commercial value as well as a visual value. Apps are probably going to be the best approach for us, which are a great way of engaging our core customers and directing them to our website.

Naturally we see a lot of brands using enormous amounts of video screens and so on, however we do also need to consider the aesthetic of our environment. Installing cutting-edge technology in an historic building would not work for us, so currently it really is a case of understanding the technology, what it can add to the business and, in particular, its content as this is a very high cost.

1

2

DISPLAY DESIGN BASICS

An understanding of basic design concepts is essential for the effective presentation of a visual concept, from store to installation. Display dynamics underpin the fundamental principles of visual merchandising and are key to creating harmonious, aesthetically pleasing displays. Learning to work with composition, colour, shape, form and pattern to achieve the best visual effect is essential for the visual merchandiser. This chapter explores how to coordinate product and display components, using a range of visual methods, to achieve a desirable outcome for the fashion retailer.

1   Simple, vertical lines create a
    strong aesthetic in this display
    at Prada.

Line

Within visually merchandised spaces, lines play an essential part in drawing the customer's eye around a space.

Vertical lines

Vertical lines are essentially straight lines that represent the shortest possible route between two points. Visual merchandising should encourage the viewer to inspect the merchandise rhythmically up and down, forcing them to open their eyes further and view more of the installation. Vertical lines can be interpreted as stabilising; however, when vertical lines are positioned diagonally they become more active and energising. V shapes are commonly used to draw the customer's attention.

Horizontal lines

Horizontal lines can be identified through the use of tables, shelves or fixtures. These add a sense of intrigue to the shopping experience by restricting the view of the product and enticing the customer to take a closer look. A more lateral approach to horizontal lines might include a reclining mannequin on a chaise longue, for example, or vinyl stripes placed on the fenestration (windows). We can use both vertical and horizontal lines to frame a window or create a focus; horizontal lines can create a relaxing effect, drawing on nature's horizon.

2
3

4

MaxMara

Circular lines

Rounded shapes are very commonly used through repetition in design. These shapes can be viewed as more feminine in contrast to sharp linear shapes and give a softer edge to a retail environment. The more curved the shape the more positive the connotations. Shapes and forms greatly affect a viewer's subconscious and touch on associations that may not be immediately recognised.

2   Horizontal lines at Prada, London.
3   Horizontal lines at Printemps, Paris.
4   Straight lines at Kenzo.
5   Vertical lines at Fenwick, London.
6   Circular Lines at ABC, New York.
7   Circular lines at Desigual.

5
6

7

Composition

Basics principles of balance and proportion are vital to successful visual merchandise display.

Symmetry

A symmetrical display is one in which the format or design is identical either side; this is otherwise known as a 'formal' display. Retailers such as John Lewis use this format to present a clean and clear product layout, making it easy to shop in a methodical and sequential way.

We can clearly see and understand how and why symmetry is often used in architecture, art and just about every other form of design; however, within product presentation the excitement can be lost. While symmetrical presentations within retail windows and spaces are the simplest form of balance, they can be a monotonous if applied everywhere.

Asymmetry

Using asymmetry in product presentation allows for more variations of balance, creating mainly off-balance presentations, which can be considered as 'informal'. In its simplest form we can use a large object placed next to a smaller one of similar type. With asymmetry we are more concerned with visual balance than whether the product is actually the same in weight, colour or texture.

Multi-asymmetry

Within one display it is possible to use a mixture of visual techniques in a more complex and creative way. A good example of a multi-asymmetrical display is shown at Bergdorf Goodman's; the double display creates dual focal points.

8

Pyramid

The pyramid is probably one of the most universally recognisable symbols, which can be identified in all areas of the art world, from sculpture and paintings to architecture, throughout history. The pyramid signifies structure, strength, balance and harmony and is often used to explain hierarchical theories. Pyramid forms are very commonly used within display; this is often the starting point for many to learn about construction in display dynamics.

Repetition

The use of repetition within product handling can be the placement of similar products at the same point or the repetition of colour, text, shape, form or texture. Andy Warhol's Marilyn Monroe screen prints are an iconic image form of repetition. This technique is used in store windows and in-store displays to create high visual impact.

8 Symmetrical window displays at Juicy Couture's flagship store on Regent Street, London.
9 Asymmetrical window display at Nike Town's Oxford Street store, London.
10 Repetition in a window display at Reed Krakoff's New York boutique.

REED KRAKOFF

Composition

Radiation

The display dynamic of radiation can be applied to a product or display configuration. Radiation can be used to create a central focal point or an off-centre focal point with a key product or visual, then products/visuals can be placed to lead from this central point, thus leading the viewer's eye outwards or across.

Step

The step is a variation on the pyramid format and can be used to show product at differing heights; normally a maximum of three steps is used. Steps (also known as podiums) may be used within a display window to achieve height and balance and make good use of space.

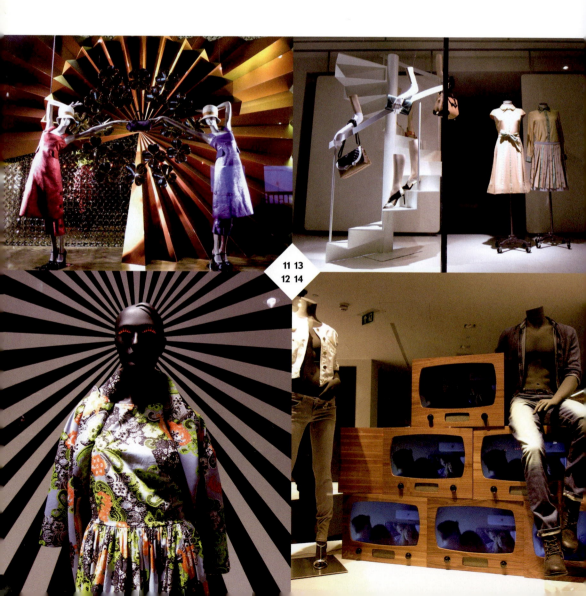

11 13
12 14

15

16

Reflection

Reflection can be a form of symmetry, such as a mirrored image. Reflection may also be used to show detail at the back of a form that would otherwise be out of the view of the customer. The technique comprises two forms, the actual and the reflected form, and it can add depth to a visual merchandising installation. A mirrored image can be very strong visually.

Contrast

Examples of contrast in visual merchandising could be through the use of contrasting shape, form, texture, line quality; the use of thick and thin, or of contrasting heights or proportion. By adding elements of contrast we break up the monotony of symmetry or repetition.

Alternation

Alternation is a variation of asymmetry and repetition. In its simplest form, alternation is the alternate repetitive placement of identical products.

Gradation

Groups of product that are similar in type but vary in size can be placed in a gradual sequence of size.

Distortion

Distortion is often used to create 'caricatures' of products, whether these are outsized and larger than life or distorted to appear as if in perspective.

11 Radiation forms the centrepiece of this Louis Vuitton holiday window display.
12 Graphics for this Fenwick display use radiation as their starting point.
13 Steps at Moschino, London.
14 TV monitors at Calvin Klein, London.
15 Angular mirrors add depth to this display at Bergdorf Goodman's New York store.
16 Mirrored baubles are used in these Burberry displays.

Composition

Proportion

Proportion can be used to good effect for small-scale products, such as perfumes and cosmetics, which may look lost in the surrounding space; props that are out of scale may then be used to show the detail.

17 19
18 20

Gravity

Gravitational installations consist of suspended or hanging elements. These can be fixed or motional, matt, shiny, textured, light, dark and so on; the main focus is that they imitate the pull of Earth gravity.

Anomaly

Introducing an anomaly or irregularity to a visual merchandising presentation can attract the interest of the customer among so many other 'like' products. There are numerous examples from which to draw inspiration, but possibly the best examples are the churches and cathedrals in Manhattan, which are often dwarfed by the uniformity and scale of the surrounding skyscrapers. Anomalies become the centre of attention when used among other products of the same type and therefore should have a specific purpose.

21

17 Selfridges, London.
18 Tiffany, London.
19 Jill Stuart, New York.
20 Theory, New York.
21 Placing props in unexpected
    positions draws attention,
    such as in this display at
    Hermes, Paris.

Texture

Surface treatments instantly provoke a response and form a central part of any visual merchandising display scheme.

Materials

A customer's response to texture is quite complex: a rough, grainy texture may look harsh whereas a smooth, silky liquid texture may encourage shoppers to touch and feel. Responses to texture play a big role in selling the product; it is evident if the consumer touches a product they are more likely to buy.

When selecting fixtures, props or mannequins it is important to relate the materials to the display scheme, brand or product. Raw materials such as metals, wood and concrete are synonymous with brands such as Diesel and All Saints. Kurt Geiger is well known for its use of reflective and mirrored surfaces for in-store shoe fixtures/fittings.

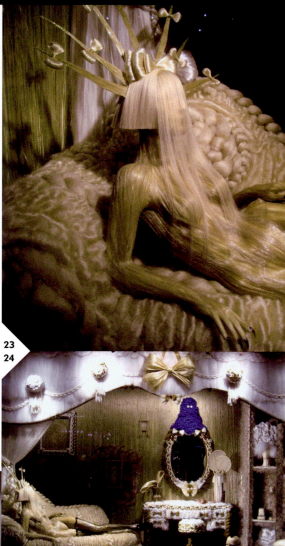

23
24

Gaga's Boudoir

22

22	Soft textures are used in Gaga's Workshop at Barneys, New York.
23-25	In these displays at Barneys, New York, hair is used to reinforce the Lady Gaga theme.
26	Hard, metal textures on display at Fendi.
27	Chrome, metallic and mirrored surfaces used in Hugo Boss, London.
28-29	Sumptuous gold textures add to the glamour of these Fendi displays.

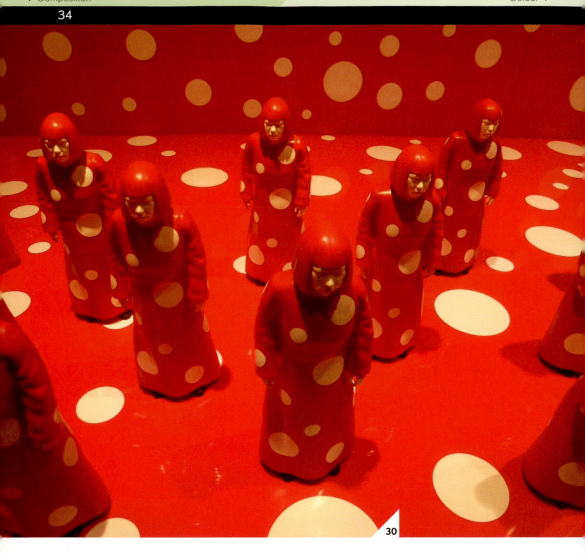

30

Pattern

The use of pattern is often driven by product and trend within visual merchandising.
A complicated pattern can bring excitement to the display, but it can easily be confusing if the mix of pattern does not work.
Geometric patterns work well as they bring a certain balance or imbalance to displays and can be distributed among product, props and mannequins.

30-32 Yayoi Kusamo for
Louis Vuitton at Selfridges
department store, London.

32

31

Rhythm

Consistency and rhythm within display has historically played a big part in retaining consumer attention. Rhythm is used to tell a story or take the customer on a journey. Rhythms can be selected to resemble an environment and duplicated in other spaces; it can be also be used as a strong navigation tool. Rhythm can be applied through colour, shape, form or pattern.

Colour

The use of colour to create visual drama and impact are one of the first design elements that a customer notices. Using colour is a cost-effective way to communicate seasonal trends, such as Christmas, sale or promotion time, and to highlight key elements within a visual merchandised area.

Using colour takes practice and skill: colour evokes emotional responses and can have cultural associations, so a basic understanding of the various dynamics is particularly important. Ultimately, the purpose of visual merchandising is to sell the product, therefore the use of colour is secondary unless it is there to enhance or support a concept. Key visual merchandising elements are shown to their best advantage when the colour used is in tune with the overall presentation, although some presentations can be made more exciting when contrasting colours are used.

33   Strong use of colour on display at Quartier 206 Department Store, Berlin.
34-35   Monochromatic colour schemes at Chanel, New York and Bergdorf Goodman, New York.

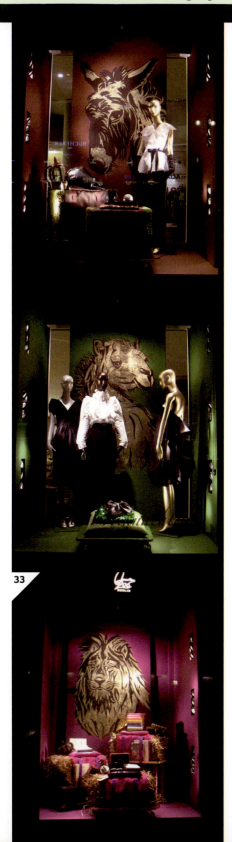

33

Dimensions and terminology of colour

Hue
Hue is the name of the colour, such as red, blue or green.

Value
The lightness or darkness of a hue is its value. Adding black, for example, produces a darker version of the colour and this is known as a shade. With each addition of black or white to a colour, its hue doesn't change, only its value.

Intensity
The saturation or purity of a colour is referred to as its intensity; it refers to its brightness or dullness. Colours are naturally most intense in their purest form.

Colour harmonies
A harmonious visual merchandising colour scheme can be accomplished by following specific rules that are based on the colour wheel.

Chromatic
High colour density such as red, blue and yellow.

Achromatic
Without colour, such as white, grey and black.

Monochromatic
Monochromatic schemes are ones that only use shades of one hue. These may be highlighted with neutrals in black or white or with the use of pattern and texture.

34 35

Colour

Analogous
Analogous visual merchandising schemes use colours that are next to each other on the colour wheel.

Complementary
This refers to colours that are on opposite sides on the colour wheel, such as red and green, blue and orange or purple and yellow.

Split complementary
We can achieve some interesting effects by using one basic colour with the two colours adjacent to the basic colour's complementary.

Double complementary
A double complement is two sets of colours or four basic colours; these must be used with care at it can be quite confusing. Possible combinations may be yellow-green, yellow-orange, blue-violet and red-violet.

Triad
Harmonious triadic hues are three main colours that are equidistant from each other on the colour wheel, such as yellow, blue and red.

Warm and cool colours
Colours have temperatures that we associate with sensations or experiences. For example, if a purple is predominantly blue it can be considered to be quite cold, whereas red, orange and yellow are considered to be warm. Consider a visual merchandising scheme to sell winter coats: cool hues, such as blue or green, would be most appropriate to create a cold atmosphere. Cool colours are often used in spaces to calm and relax, leading to higher energy levels. Warm colours psychologically make us hungry, so they are often used in restaurants.

Advancing and receding colours
There is a sense that some colours advance while other recede. When viewing colours from a distance the warm hues, such as red and orange (advancing colours) seem to appear nearer than their cold counterparts, such as greens and blues (receding hues). A pale, less intense hue may be used to create the effect of visually enlarging a space. Alternatively, to achieve a more cosy feeling then a bright orange may be used to bring the walls in.

36 THE COLOUR WHEEL

The colour wheel is used as the basis for all colour theory.

36

Shades
Shades of hues are achieved by adding black.

Tints
Adding white to a hue creates a tint. It is important to consider the various principles of colour theory; so for tints to be equal on the colour wheel, equal amounts of white or black will be added.

Multicoloured
A mix of colours can be used together to create interesting and ambiguous colour combinations.

Dominant
A dominant hue is the use of one hue in large proportion. Dominant hues are used to add drama and create a visual statement, which perhaps highlights the main trend of the season.

Highlight or accents
Highlight or accent colours are used to break up the monotony of one or two combination colours. This technique can work very well against a black, white and grey (achromatic scheme), injecting life and activity and emphasising an area in a store.

Colour

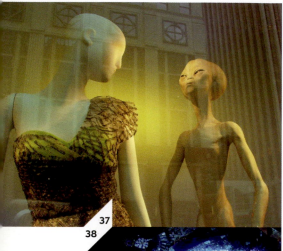

37

38

Neutrals

These colours can be mixed or placed with any other colour in the spectrum. Often used by buyers for core fashion lines as these colours are easily worn: navy, black, white, beige and brown.

Brights

The most intense primary colours, which are strong in attraction.

Pastels

Colours with added white to wash the intensity, making them softer in appearance.

Mid-tones

Not bright, not pastel but in between these in colour density.

Jewel tones

Regal, precious stone colours such as ruby, emerald and amethyst.

Muted tones

Dusty colours with grey added.

Earth tones

A collection of natural colours such as rust and sand; these can be rich in appearance and may have a warm autumnal look.

39

37 Different levels of atmospherics acheived through creative use of colour and lighting at Bergdorf Goodman, New York.
38 Bergdorf Goodman, New York.
39 Colour intensity at Harvey Nichols, London.

Associations and emotional effects

Scientific research has shown colours to
have a direct emotional effect. It is therefore
important to use colour not only to attract
consumers but to also create a pleasurable
experience. People have instant associations
of colour with brands or products, such
as the strong duck-egg blue of jewellery
designers Tiffany; the dark green and gold
of Harrods or the red tab of Levi's denim.
Selecting the right hue is integral to the
success and visual dominance of a product,
company or a brand in today's competitive
retail environment. When using colour in a
space, the dimensions and scale of colour
need to be considered, as well as the activity
of the shoppers.

Purple
Regal, prestigious and special, purple
is historically a sacred colour. Purple is
calming, uplifts the mood and can
enhance spirituality. It has both warm
and cool properties and can be used to
create a relaxing and calming effect in
selected surroundings.

Blue
Light and cool blues can be serene and
cooling. Blue is a safe, loyal colour and one
of the most popular colours in the world.
Associated with the colour of the sea,
sky and the universe, its alliance with water
means it is associated with cleanliness and
masculinity. However to feel 'blue' is to
feel sad.

Green
Green has a soothing effect, good for
learning and calming environments, and has
eco-friendly associations.

Black
Western symbolisation of mourning, the
colour of authority. Associated with evil,
tragedy and illnesses such as the plague.

Red
This colour has high intensity and energy;
it is used to good effect in exercise rooms
and restaurants as it stimulates hunger. It
denotes anger and passion and is the colour
most associated with seasonal sales in the
retail environment.

Yellow
Many product offers are advertised in yellow
because it stands out in the colour spectrum.
This mood-enhancing colour speaks
confidence and boosts clarity of thought.

White
International sign of surrender, purity and
newness in the West.

Cultural associations of colour

Visual merchandising designers need
to be sensitive to powerful associations
with colours, such as colours of political
parties, cultural symbolism and personal
instinctive meaning. Wrongly translating
colour meanings in different countries can
be detrimental to a retail business trading in
international markets. For example, purple
denotes death in some Asian countries
and red represents the colour of prosperity
in China.

Lighting

Coloured lighting is often used on the high street to help support the brand message or to promote a product or event. This technique involves the use of coloured filters or gels, available in a multitude of colours, which are wrapped around fluorescent tubes. Care should be taken that the filters do not distort the colour of the actual product, but are used to enhance the commercial environment and the customer experience. These techniques are highly effective in the art of window display.

Exterior lighting

Exterior lighting may be applied to an external commercial space to give drama and attract the customer from a long distance, in light boxes, video walls or window lighting, for example. This may be decorative or used to highlight particular products.

Interior lighting

Interior lighting should be functional but can also be decorative. Lighting effects can be used to create drama or to highlight specific areas.

Accent lighting is used to provide a balance with general lighting. Retailers with greater emphasis on overall luminance usually require very little accent lighting. Types of accent lighting include spotlights, halogen lights and high-intensity discharge lamps. Distance between the product and the light source should be considered: the greater the distance, the lesser the effect.

40 Effective lighting in a
New York store window display.

Interview: Patrick Minkley, Anthropologie

Patrick Minkley, originally from Los Angeles, is District Visual Manager for Anthropologie. He works with a small team on all types of visual display.

Q **How did you get into the industry?**

A One autumn after university, I was jobless after quitting an unpleasant graphic design job. Feeling it would at least be something creative, I took a temporary position on the display team at a department store, helping out with Christmas display preparations. Before I knew it, I was in full-time. Within a year, I became a visual manger of my own store and have worked my way forward ever since.

Q **What do you love about working in visual merchandising?**

A The retail world is constantly changing and evolving. Working in visual merchandising provides the challenge and opportunity to keep current and be true to your brand. I love absorbing newness in design, product and culture, then translating it to make it appropriate for our environment. My job keeps my senses alert and also reflects my personal interests. It's a win-win situation!

Q **How does a new scheme development begin?**

A We have an amazing, small team of people in our home office who help pull together visual merchandising big ideas and influences for each season. They not only work closely with the product designers and buyers, but gather input and inspiration from the field and store level as well. It is extremely collaborative on all levels.

Interview: Patrick Minkley, Anthropologie

Q Where do you go to generate new ideas?

A Personally, I can be inspired in many ways – not only by the expected, in art galleries or imagery from magazines and blogs, but in observing and absorbing life all around us. Ideas can spark from anywhere if you take time to look long enough, or just notice details. Travelling, exploring and putting yourself in new situations or environments helps heighten and sharpen the senses.

Q How do you decide what needs to be produced?

A One of the best attributes of Anthropologie is that all of the displays are hand-made in store by the visual teams. It's something that most retailers cannot claim and what sets us apart. This approach truly honours the individual creativity that each employee brings to their role and the stores. Every environment and display is tailored specifically to each store.

Q What are some of the newest trends?

A I have an aversion to the word 'trend', but I suppose everything has a peak of popularity at some point in its lifecycle. Some of the newest trends are actually old ones recycled again from years past. Some trends aren't necessarily of great design or importance, but have reached a level of popular aesthetics through other means. Ultimately, I think a balance of being true to yourself with an injection of current trend is best, whether that is personally or as a retailer.

Q How do you think you became so successful in your role?

A I think success comes from patience, dedication and being open to learn in any way. There is always something new to experience in any situation. Remembering successes and opportunities from your past is also key in moving forward to make better decisions or take new approaches in the future. Lastly, I truly believe that when your personal life interests are very similar to what you do at work, things come naturally, and ideas and thoughts are ongoing.

Q What kinds of themes and materials do you produce?

A The visual teams in each store plan, produce and execute all aspects of the visual merchandising. They set the floor plan, create merchandising narratives through the product, then design and create display to support and enhance that. All materials are sourced individually according to their specific needs and budgets.

Q Is sustainability an important part of your development process?

A We always strive to create displays from innovative and either recycled or recyclable materials. We often keep costs down by reinventing and reinterpreting supplies from previous displays or look at how an 'unwanted' material can become something beautiful. Things that cannot be reused will be donated to organisations, schools or auctioned for charities. Connecting to our customers and communities in new ways through display is an ongoing focus for us.

SPACE PLANNING PRINCIPLES

3

In this chapter we look at the customer journey to and within the physical retail space. What are the various characteristics and components that help create a visually stimulating environment into which the customer is enticed and encouraged to shop? The various 'layers' such as store windows, fixtures, graphics, lighting are critically important, as is maximising store layout. With such an enormous variety of choice on the high streets around the world, the various principles of visual merchandising must work to create the desire to purchase.

In fashion retailing, a product can be a luxury item and not something that is needed to survive, but simply wanted and desired. Once a customer has been encouraged to visit the store we need to consider how we orientate them, help them navigate through the space, place 'like' products together and maximise sales opportunities while creating a pleasant shopping experience so that they return again.

1   Desigual's New York store has a painted exterior.

Store architecture and retail formats

The most important factor for any retailer is to define its product and inform its customers of the product ranges and available choices. While visual merchandising is used to attract customers, it is also necessary to define a brand's image and encourage brand loyalty by creating a pleasurable and memorable shopping experience. Key indicators include:

× Architecture of the store
× Website
× Store layout
× Windows (or lack of)
× Symbols
× Props
× Signage
× Promotional activities
× Lighting
× Sound
× Smell
× Graphics

The role of visual merchandising on the high street begins with the exterior of the store. The facade and building are often underestimated in terms of impact and customer experience and yet this is the first impression of the brand.

The selection or design of the retail building can reflect a brand's values and personality; communicating its exterior identity will aid the potential customer's decision process. While some retail spaces are exclusively designed (such as Louis Vuitton's 'Maison' on London's Bond Street, which was famously designed by architect Peter Marino), retail buildings are more often inherited, challenging the retail store designer to redesign and reinvent the shell of an existing space. In particular, consideration needs to be given to the size of the space, its location, product range and customer profile, which all affect the style formats and planning of the space.

Store types

Department stores, flagship stores, multi-brand retailers, independents, boutique shops and high street retailers all demand specific visual merchandising strategies, which need to reflect and reinforce the brand style of the retailer within the limitations of its retail space.

2   A typical mall setting.
3   Alberta Ferretti store, London.
4   Burlington Arcade, London.
5   Dior store, Paris.
6   Storefront for Camper, London.
7   Pop-up designer shop in Berlin.
8   Swarovski pop-up store in New York.
9   Uniqlo, New York.

2 3

4 5
6 7

8 9

Store architecture and retail formats

Locations

Different architecture styles add character and project a sense of historic relevance and authenticity to a brand, often within a mixed contemporary shopping landscape.

Flagship stores

The flagship store is a retailer's primary location and largest commercial selling space; it is usually a store in a prominent part of a large city and it is distinct from the rest of the chain. Flagships are usually where a retailer tests and tries new concepts before they are rolled out across the rest of the chain. These stores also hold the highest volume of merchandise, cater for a wider variety of customers and present the best opportunities and largest budgets for visual merchandisers to produce exciting concepts.

Characteristics of flagship stores

× Iconic or dominant architecture and store design
× Larger sized store
× Premium location
× Exclusive product range
× Extensive range availability
× First store to launch
× Highest footfall
× Exceptional service available, exceeding customer expectations
× Product previews, events and promotions
× Specialist in particular area of merchandise
× Leading in display innovation, using technology to its best advantage in retail space

10 Ralph Lauren's women's flagship store stands proud on Madison Avenue, New York and was built to replicate the existing men's flagship store across the road. The same materials were used in keeping with the architecture of the men's store.

11 Topshop flagship, Oxford Circus, London.
12 Topman General Store, London.
13 Louis Vuitton flagship, New York.
14 Louis Vuitton flagship, London.

11 12

One brand can take on different styles of store architecture depending on location, environment, customer and climate. For example Topman has a flagship store on Oxford Circus in central London, but have opened a different version of Topman in an urban East London location. Designed for the local trendy and artistic set, Topman General Store could be mistaken for a vintage or second-hand outlet. An understated, hand-crafted approach to window design profiles this concept store away from Topman's usual multiple chain identity. Exposed brick walls, reclaimed vintage furniture, graphic montages and handmade signage decorate the interior surfaces, with not a hint of mass production in sight. This store redefines and repositions the brand within a more intimate fashion elite market.

In the iconic London flagship Louis Vuitton 'Maison', gold brand logos are suspended in the windows and inlaid in the flooring. Materials such as Corian, dichroic glass, wood inlaid with gold leaf, gold titanium shelves and ochre coloured carpets forge a strong link between the world of luxury retailing and the exclusive shopping experience. This central London emporium offers more than any other Louis Vuitton store, such as a book gallery section and artworks by British artists. There is a private shopping area located on the top floor, which is exclusive to very important shoppers. An LED staircase runs through the three floors of luxury, displaying different coloured lights and moving digital imagery.

13 14

Space hierarchy

Effective space management is fundamental to the success of a store. Basic space planning principles are used to monitor sales, space performance and analysis, in order to assess if the space is actually working in terms of profit or not. The benefits of effective store layout are:

× To maximise sales and increase profit
× Promote specific products
× Manipulate customer flow
× Efficient use of space

As visual merchandisers we are constantly challenged by the aesthetics of our installations and their value in terms of sales. Addressing the space hierarchy helps to justify a visual strategy to the more commercial side of the business.

Beginning with an empty store

The task of designing a store layout can be an exciting project, with merchandisers, buyers and the commercial team all working together to communicate the brand identity. Once presented with an architectural plan, a store audit and evaluation should take place to observe the following visual details:

× Sources of natural light – people instinctively prefer to spend time in naturally lit spaces so it's important to try to preserve some.
× Entrances and exits – to ascertain the main footfall and start planning high traffic areas within the store.
× Architectural oddities – recesses, beams and structural elements that can be worked with to design the space or worked against to redefine the space.
× Lifts and escalators – these transitory areas act as entrances and exits and can add value to surrounding space.
× Windows – the location of windows determines the relevance and importance of product placement and scheme.
× Sightlines – the customer's view into and around a store. This is a useful way of prioritising the key areas of the retail environment.
× Focal points – these are positioned at the end of a sightline in the form of a graphic, a display of product, props and so on.
× Pause points – these are usually a fixture or display of product that encourage the customer to stop and browse or buy; an essential way to break up long walkways or large areas of space.

Using zones to determine the value of a space will help in planning a store more effectively.

15 Sightlines.
16 Focal points.
17 Hierarchy of space.
18 Hierarchy of space with the addition of a cash desk; note the changes to value in selling space.

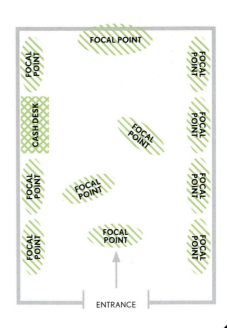

CASH DESK

ENTRANCE

15

FOCAL POINT

FOCAL POINT

FOCAL POINT

CASH DESK

FOCAL POINT

FOCAL POINT

FOCAL POINT

FOCAL POINT

FOCAL POINT

FOCAL POINT

FOCAL POINT

ENTRANCE

16

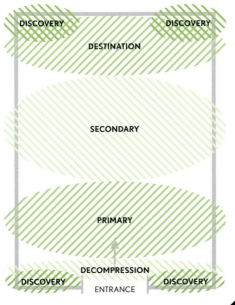

DISCOVERY   DISCOVERY

DESTINATION

SECONDARY

PRIMARY

DECOMPRESSION

DISCOVERY   ENTRANCE   DISCOVERY

17

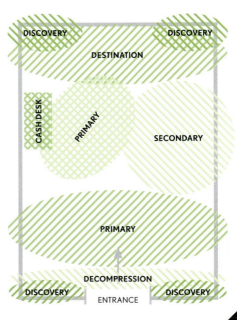

DISCOVERY   DISCOVERY

DESTINATION

CASH DESK

PRIMARY

SECONDARY

PRIMARY

DECOMPRESSION

DISCOVERY   ENTRANCE   DISCOVERY

18

Space hierarchy

Decompression space

The first few feet of a store are often referred to as the decompression zone, an entry area customers use to 'decompress' or adjust to the new space. The decompression zone is not a valuable selling space as the customer often looks up ahead as they are walking into the store, overlooking any product or displays positioned too close to the entrance.

Primary space

This begins just beyond the threshold space. It is excellent prime selling space and gains the most footfall (customers walking through). Primary selling space can also be located at other entrances such as tops of escalators, stairs and in front of cash desks, where there is an impulse selling opportunity. Clothing stores usually position their fast-selling high fashion lines within this space, where the turnover of product is naturally higher.

Secondary space

This is good selling space where fashion retailers present their core essentials or 'bread and butter' lines. These lines have a good profit margin and complement the higher end, seasonal fashion lines.

Destination space

This is located towards the rear of the store, but is visible from the front or midway point. This space acts as a kind of 'umbrella', taking up the perimeter wall bay for maximum visibility to lure customers to the back of the store. Denim, shoes or accessories sections tend be located here as customers navigate their way in a more purposeful destination shop.

Discovery space

This is the space within the front and back corners of the store where customers do not naturally migrate. It can be very difficult to sell much from this space, but it can be used for sale merchandise (when not trading in full sale), broken lines or ranges that are incomplete.

Perimeter walls

The wall space of a store is generally the second best selling space available. Visibility points are valuable and have good sightline and focal point opportunities. The perimeter walls can be merchandised to full height or up to the lighting level. Walls can feature a mixture of signage, graphics, imagery, colour, lighting, product, props and fixtures.

Transitional selling space

This space needs to reflect the customer's mindset at different times of year. It needs to be flexible for seasonal and transitional lines and tends to be located within the most commercially rewarding, primary selling area of the store. Phasing of stock will depend on the number of core lines or the product lifecycle.

Special selling strategies

Impulse merchandising

Impulse purchases tend be those products that the customer had not planned to buy before entering the store. For this reason, cosmetics are always positioned at the front of department stores. Retailers maximise this strategy by placing smaller products, such as accessories, near cash desks so that queuing shoppers will be enticed to add more to their shopping baskets.

19 Transitional selling space and destination positioning.
20 Impulse layout.

Outpost merchandising

Outpost merchandising is used to promote a specific product. Some stores use this strategy to engage with the customer mindset or to promote seasonal products, by placing key products in the aisles or front of departments.

Last chance to buy

This type of merchandise is grouped on one fixture with a temporary feel. The advantage for the visual merchandiser and retailer is that it keeps the rest of the store clean, without end-of-line items interrupting fresh collections. For customers, it enables them to browse pieces that could otherwise be hard to find in store, and creates a sense of urgency to buy 'last chance' items. This fixture should be placed close to the cash desk or towards the back of the store.

Customer mindset merchandising

Reacting to the local market is becoming ever more important. Even within a multinational retailer that directs product placement from head office, it is important to make some tweaks and take into account local decision-making without compromising the look of the brand. A simple example of this would be to bring the umbrellas to the front of the store when it's raining. This is a simple, traditional method of visual merchandising that should tap into the customer's mindset when shopping.

SALE DESTINATION

TRANSITIONAL SELLING SPACE (SEASONAL, HOLIDAY, CHRISTMAS, NEW LINES ETC.)

ENTRANCE

19

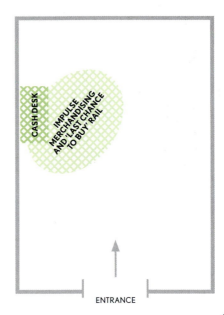

CASH DESK

IMPULSE MERCHANDISING AND 'LAST CHANCE TO BUY' RAIL

ENTRANCE

20

Space planning layouts

Space management at both macro and micro level has a huge impact on the customer's shopping experience and the commercial performance of a store. Communicating a clearly defined retail brand identity, reflecting the requirements of the target market and providing consumer choice are the main goals of any retailer. Over time, retailers have developed several basic floor plan layouts in order to maximise the movement of customers past the maximum number of fixtures in the minimum amount of time. The right store layout will set the overall visual appearance of the brand but it is equally important to consider the aesthetic of the commercial space and the customer's comfort. Interior presentation layouts can be addressed in the following ways.

Simple grid layout

Commonly used in supermarket environments or stores that stock items in bulk, this layout features the positioning of fixtures and/or displays in rows or grids. Products are easy to find, and it is easy to plan and maintain the layout. Several main walkways are positioned front to back of store and side to side.

Loop layout

Department stores often approach their large trading spaces with a loop walkway, similar to a racing track. This exposes the customer to a greater variety of products as they navigate their way around the departments. The loop acts as a viewing point from which consumers can see departments and decide where to enter. They will also be guided by graphics and sightlines. Popular Swedish home furnishing chain IKEA has multiple loops within its 'yellow brick road' navigation. Whilst this is favoured by many, it can be a shopping nightmare for the destination shopper who does not wish to browse around the store; fortunately there are occasional 'break' points or shortcuts along the route.

21 Simple grid layout.
22 Loop fashion layout.
23 Flexible grouping layout.
24 Exhibition layout.

walkway

shelving

rail

mannequin

tables

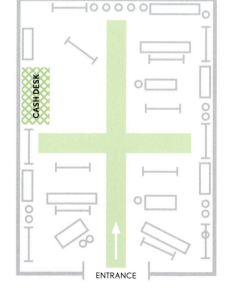

21

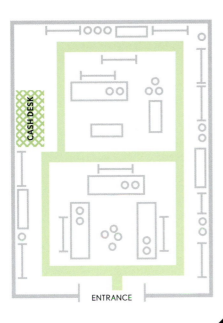

Flexible grouping layout

Fashion retailers embrace this type of layout because it increases flexibility and accessibility; additions or reductions in merchandise collections can also be made easily. This informal layout encourages shoppers to browse and move freely between different departments, exposing them to a wider variety of merchandise. Fixtures, mannequins, signage and props can all be changed and fixtures merchandised with a freestyle approach.

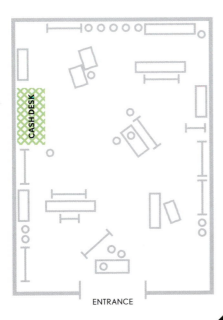

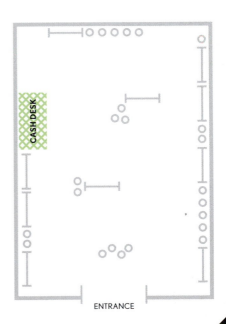

Space planning layouts

The exhibition layout

The exhibition or gallery layout is usually adopted by luxury fashion retailers, whereby the perimeter of the store is predominantly used to display merchandise, while the floor space is kept clear for customers to circulate easily. This is one format where empty floor space is actually favoured, emulating that of an exhibition space where the product becomes the work of art. Providing spaces for customers to think, relax, socialise and breathe is a high priority. This layout achieves maximum visibility because there are no barriers in front of the merchandise. Only very important pieces are displayed, with maybe only a few sizes on view, but a personalised customer service waits nearby. Louis Vuitton, Stella McCartney and McQueen are a few examples of retailers that use the exhibition layout style.

The island layout

Boutiques and independent fashion stores that are short of space tend to create islands in the centre of the store, which become focal points for product or promotions. Using an eye-level fixture or lower fixture such as a table, the island can be shopped from all angles and as such is heavily stocked at the front, back and sides. A walkway either side of the island encourages the customer to move in a figure-of-eight around the store.

Combined layouts

Mixed formats of all the aforementioned layouts can be used to zone areas, to communicate a different type of product category or to change the customer's shopping pace within larger stores.

Concession layouts

Larger retailers and department stores often contain concession spaces rented by other brands. Each space is treated as an individual store with its own identified focal points, sightlines, graphics and props, and merchandise layout. Top-selling or trend items are usually placed to face the customer traffic flow or within prime selling spaces to encourage the shopper in.

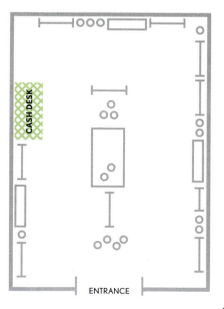

CASH DESK

ENTRANCE

25

Sale product layout

With the exception of some luxury brands, sale items are a necessary part of the retail cycle. Beyond the usual sale period, items that have been reduced to clear are usually placed at the back of the store. Some retailers with a multi-brand portfolio may gather all sale or clearance items and sell them in out-of-town outlet stores or shopping villages away from their main retail spaces.

Balance between product and non-selling spaces

Luxury brands tend to display fewer products on the shop floor whereas value retailers tend to have a 'pile them high, sell them cheap' attitude to trading. The quantity of space allocated to product and non-product spaces is determined by the fashion brand values, market level, the individual customer's needs, the type of services available at the store and, ultimately, the type of product offering. Examples of non-selling space include other services such as rest areas, space for pushchairs, wheelchairs or entertainment areas.

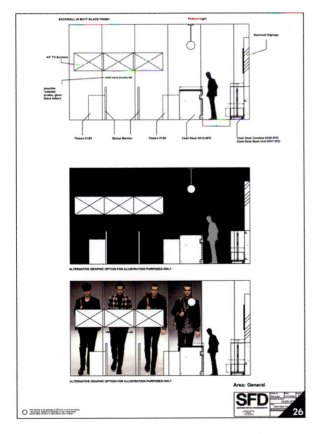

25 Island layout.
26 Cash desk specification drawings.

Customer navigation

Customers can be led through the store by main walkways mapped out by fixture configurations or flooring designs. Orientation is designated by fixture layout, store signage, graphics, props and zoning of space. Sightlines, focal points and pause points are carefully plotted along the customer journey, with key products highlighted along the way. Adjacencies in product type or style should be mapped carefully to avoid interrupting the flow of the store layout; this enables the customer to navigate smoothly around the store space.

Circulation space

Circulation space is determined by fixtures, in-store visual merchandising and designated pathways that are purposefully mapped out to allow heavier traffic to move quickly into a store rather than single file customers walking at a slower pace. Larger pathways are mainly used in big format stores; smaller stores may use only one or two main walkways or none at all, with many more circulation paths in between fixtures. This allows customers to meander around the merchandise at their own pace.

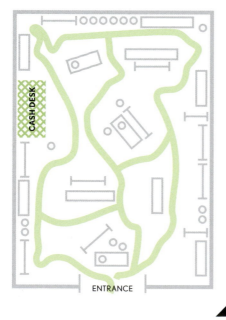

CASH DESK

ENTRANCE

27

27 Selling strategies: circulation space.
28 Floor plan with fixtures.

28

Customer navigation

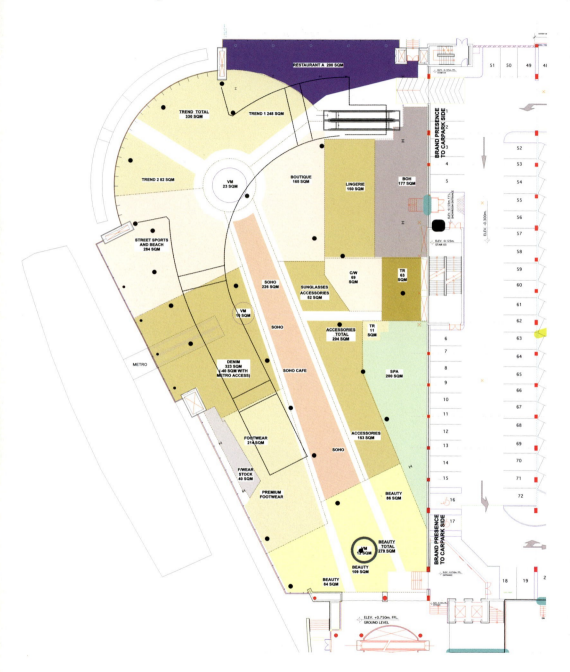

29 Floor plan with zoned areas.

Walkways

Defining walkways serves to guide customers in the preferred direction and it can be achieved by using a different type of flooring from the sales areas. It is effective in enticing a 'non-committal' or 'nervous' customer, who may perceive the walkway as a physical barrier into a department or space. Open-plan stores often adopt universal flooring throughout, relying instead on in-store visual merchandising, signage and fixtures to create walkways and flow.

Cash desks and changing rooms

It is practical commercially to position cash desks and changing rooms in areas that are less profitable, which is why they are usually situated towards the back of a store. The area surrounding the cash desk is also perfect for the placement of impulse buys.

Planograms

A planogram is a diagram or an image of an area within a retail space, used to communicate to multiple sites and/or calculate the potential sales that can be generated. Planograms are used by buyers, merchandisers, visual merchandisers and sales staff to gather product data, such as the type and quantity of merchandise, product name, supplier, brand, cost and so on, as well as to support the mapping of store merchandise. They are particularly useful to visual merchandisers within larger, multiple brand retailers because they illustrate the type of fixture required and how the product should be laid out to maintain brand equity across a variety of stores. The retailer will usually dictate how much product is placed depending on the sales targets. Product is often merchandised in order to simplify purchase and replenishment, particularly in fast fashion environments.

Fashion concessions

Fashion concessions are essentially a mini store within a store. A luxury brand will normally have its own kit of parts or shop fit, whereas smaller brands may simply have an in-store fixture or branded structure from which merchandise is sold. These mini stores provide a slightly more specialist service and therefore need to stand out from the rest of the store. Very often these spaces may be enclosed, with different levels of lighting and different flooring, as well as their own branded look.

Fashion services

Many contemporary fashion retailers offer additional services in store to enhance the customer experience and ultimately to keep them there as long as possible to spend more money. Services range from hairdressers, nail bars, cafés, alterations, events, gift-wrapping, shoe repairs, body piercing and tattooists to personal shopping and styling. These additional services encourage social scenarios and interaction, which helps to build on the brand equity and increase the likelihood of impulse purchases.

Journey to sale

Journey to sale refers to product or service advertising either on or in a store. Historically, graphics were used in the commercial environment as a form of communication and even today we are able to find direct links between old traditional signage and contemporary retail, such as the red-and-white barber's pole, for example.

Journey to sale 'elements' or 'indicators' within contemporary retailing are created to specifically target and entice the customer into the retail environment. Early forms of graphics and signage were painted on the fenestration of retailers at the beginning of the 19th century. With the invention of plate glass and subsequently neon lighting during the early 20th century, store branding was usually sent to the retailers from the product manufacturers and printed on metal sheets to display in store or on the building itself. The success of any advertising campaign is measured by the sales revenue generated and is often tied in with national or international campaigns in magazines and newspapers or television and cinema. Today's advertising carries fairly informal images and promotional messages designed to quickly capture consumer attention in a highly mobile, design literate and technology driven society.

30 Directional signage at
Ben Sherman store, London.

30

Journey to sale

Types of signage

Materials used at the end of the customer journey vary, but may often be a stand-alone sign that leads the customer to the selling space or it may even be a part of the architecture. Journey to sale can begin with advertising on:

× Transport, such as lorries, vans, cars, buses, aeroplanes, taxis, livery vans
× Wall covers
× Painted graphics
× Video walls
× Decorated sheds
× Promotional vinyl
× Show cases
× Totem pole signage
× Banners
× Projecting illuminated signage
× Fascia signage
× Pavement signage
× Chalk boards
× Changeable sandwich boards

In addition, they can be in the form of:

× Promotional displays (used for the duration of a particular campaign usually with a short life expectancy and made from cardboard or plastic)
× Permanent displays (such as those at airports, for example)
× Packaging
× Retail store windows
× Posters / billboards
× Signage (in-store directional signage and fascia)
× The retail environment
× Hoardings (built as a safety cover around an entrance during construction)

31

31 Signage on the walls of Hollister's New York store.
32 Desigual's New York store has a painted exterior.

32

Identification signage

Identification signage is usually contained within a particular department signifying to the customer that they are entering a particular space. This type of signage may be changed quite often as departments are moved or re-merchandised, so it is often produced for temporary use.

Call to action signage

Call to action signage is usually the last part of the customer's journey to sale, at least in terms of persuading the customer to part with their cash. This type of signage is usually in the form of 'buy it now and receive a discount' variety or a BOGOF (i.e., buy one, get one free).

Tickets

Ticketing and communicating the cost of a product is inevitably the last opportunity to persuade a customer to buy. With a fantastic window scheme and an amazing interior, all of the sightlines and focal points considered, and fixtures and graphics in place, this is the moment to close the deal. With fashion merchandise the pricing is generally understated (unless it is part of a promotion) and it is up to the customer, after being persuaded by the celebrity endorsement, a current promotion or peer approval, to decide whether or not they wish to buy the product.

Directional signage

Any signage used within commercial spaces needs to 'tell it like it is', to be clear, concise, to the point and big enough to be seen and read, particularly across a large and busy retail environment. Some retailers illuminate their signage or install flashing neon signs. Larger stores have enquiry desks from which store maps can be collected and directions given on a one-to-one basis. However it is implemented, the signage should work with the brand image.

Case study: Chameleon Visual

Overview

Chameleon Visual is a London based design company that produces and installs bespoke projects for fashion environments. Clients of the company have included the luxury fashion brands Louis Vuitton, Theo Fennell, Christian Louboutin, and Hermes as well as famous department stores, Harrods and Selfridges. Chameleon Visual also produces campaigns for major London events such as London Fashion Week. The company creates exciting and innovative projects from concept to completion, taking their clientele through the design process from initial briefing through to handing over of the final outcomes to the highest specifications.

The project

Chameleon Visual was asked to develop and curate an exhibition for Matches Fashion at London Fashion Week, to 'support and nurture talent wherever possible in their home city'. The project needed to be multimedia in order to highlight Matches' various platforms - from store to online, to mobile and magazine. The objectives of the project were:

× To showcase a newly curated selection of British luxury fashion brands within a temporary structural space.
× To hold a public relations event for the London Fashion press and the general public for London Fashion Week.
× To create a temporary installation celebrating the best of London luxury fashion that could be emulated around the world and increase their presence as a luxury boutique.

INITIAL SKETCHES AND IDEAS

The Chameleon design team at work, floor planning and concept-building for Matches store, London.

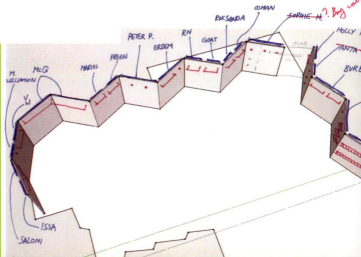

The process

The general process of the development of a new commission often begins with either a phone call from a client or an email enquiry which the team follow up by arranging a face to face meeting.

During these meetings the team have the opportunity to discuss:

× The potential of a project
× What a client requires of the company
× The budget that a client has to spend
× Possibly constraints of what the client wishes to achieve
× The lead times for a project
× The issuing of a brief or taking a brief from a client
× Production of hand drawn sketches
× Client requesting specific elements for a launch of a project or a new concept
× Mindstorming sessions with the client
× Production of schemes based around current products (product led development)
× Seasonal trends

Initial development

Chameleon Visual obtained plans, sections and elevations of the site from the architectural practice who worked on the initial Matches store development. The team needed to ensure that all measurements were accurate by surveying the space themselves as a precautionary procedure. Once the team were confident that they had their own accurate drawings they were able to begin overlaying these with sketches.

The team worked through a variety of store layouts in order maximise the selling space and reinforce the various brands being curated for the nine-day event. A free flow layout was decided because of the advantage that this layout offers. Once the team had designed and developed a series of possible solutions for the existing space, these were presented formally to the Matches senior management team.

Case study: Chameleon Visual

Design and installation

The winning solution involved designing an outsized box of matches, from which pages were unfolding. These were produced as a series of inter-connecting, angled vertical panels running the periphery of the retail space. The completed panels were sprayed in a white satin 2-pac finish prior to installation. Once installed the white satin vertical panels were then punctuated with 24 carat gold hand plated rails from which to hang the merchandise.

As the Matches brand carries all luxury merchandise, it was absolutely necessary to consider every element which was to be installed in minutiae detail. On each of the white panels, the names of each of the luxury brand fashion houses were added in order to direct the customer to the relevant panel. The team also developed and designed white matchboxes in which jewellery could be presented. The brand names of the designers were added to the front of these, as well as the wall fixtures and podiums.

COMPUTER RENDERINGS OF THE MATCHBOX IDEA

Signage, lighting and display tables are all detailed in these renderings.

Installation of the scheme was quite a lengthy process. As most inherited building structures including floors are not absolutely perfectly at 90 degree angles, some panels needed additional cuts to be made in order to make them fit closer. This is a perfectly normal procedure and the reason that specialists are employed for installation of a scheme. Once the site had been prepared, electricians, carpenters, a vinyl team and visual merchandisers with specialist skills arrived on site in order to prepare for the temporary structures installation.

Mannequins were also placed and secured onto small mdf podiums with a white satin two-pack finish and the name of the individual designer applied to them by the vinyl team.

Once everything had been installed on site to the highest specifications expected of a luxury brand the cleaning and polishing process began. Any fine details that needed attention or 'snagging' were identified and immediately rectified. Only once everything was in place did the handover to the client begin.

THE FINAL SCHEME INSTALLED

Shopfitters on-site, and the final collections on display.

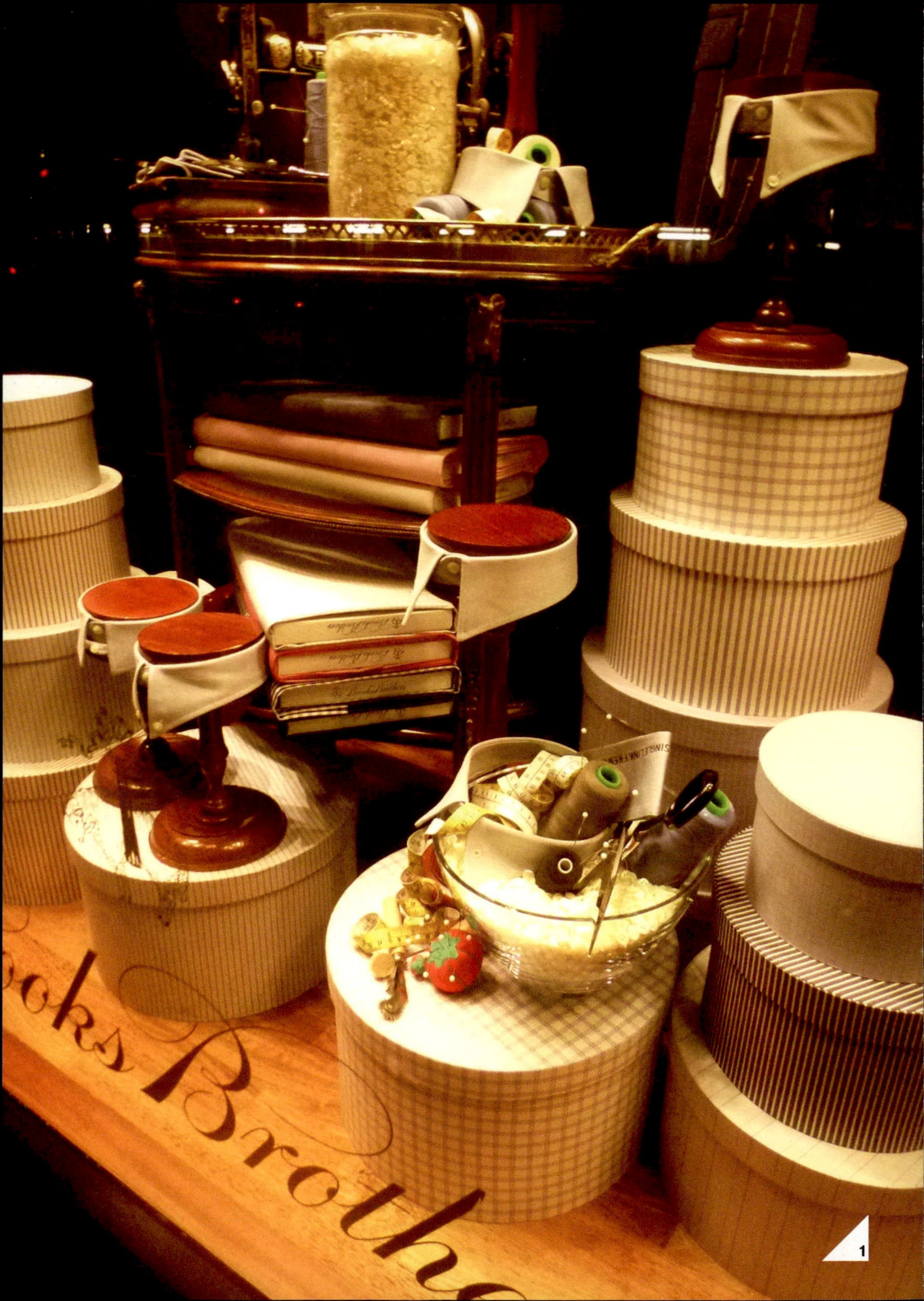

1

4

DISPLAYING MERCHANDISE

Consideration of the parameters of space within the physical retail environment is essential in creating the shopper's journey and maximising points of visual inspiration at every opportunity. Designing a visual merchandising concept or scheme is just the beginning of the process. This chapter identifies the complexities of initiating 3D production and installation in order to understand how to generate the optimum realisation of creative ideas within the selling space.

1   Props and packaging on display at
    Brooks Brothers, London.

Retail windows

Historically store windows were designed to enable customers to view the retailer's offer before entering. In contemporary retailing this comprehensive selling space has a more complex commercial context. Store windows can entertain, engage and inspire the consumers, helping them to build an association and relationship with the retail brand.

A window is like the cover of a book: the design, style, content and narrative should entice the viewer inside. When designing store windows the visual merchandiser needs to consider the message and how this will engage the customer or passer-by. Most retailers are aware that windows can be used as visual PR. It is also crucial to continue the window themes in store, which helps to create visual cohesion and project a clear brand message.

Fashion window formats

Window styles are determined by store profile and the nature of the brand. They are often inherited spaces, depending on whether the store is newly built or an historical building.

Access

Access and size of window space are one of the first aspects to consider. Closed-back windows, for example, tend to have an access door hidden from the customer's view. In some instances the back walls come away to enable access for large props, graphics or digital media.

Space

The size of the window space is also critical in design and planning terms, whether the space is large or small, deep or shallow, high or low and how the display will be viewed: from the front, side, back or from multiple angles. Other factors include the placement of electricity points, how the window space will be painted and how it will be maintained.

Open back

The open-back window format allows the customer to see the interior of store from outside and equally, from the inside out. The main consideration for the visual merchandiser is that the products can be seen from a three-dimensional perspective. This format enables greater connection between the products and the retail space.

2

Closed back

Closed-back windows are typical of traditional retailers, often containing theatrical schemes with backdrops, props and lighting that focus on the narrative. Larger retailers, such as department stores, may use this format to create sequential displays or design themes across multiple windows. Sequential windows showcasing a theme can tell a story in visual chapters.

Half back

Half-back windows tend to be used in smaller, speciality stores. Graphics are often hung in order to differentiate the interior space from the window scheme and the products, which are changed on a regular basis.

Corner window

Corner windows gain more exposure as they are visible from two or more streets. Often the schemes are more complex because the viewing points and sightlines are in multiple directions; here, side views are just as important as frontal display.

2   Open-backed window at Mulberry.
3   Closed back window at Hugo Boss.
4   Half-back windows at Todds.
5   Corner window at Massimo Dutti.

Retail windows

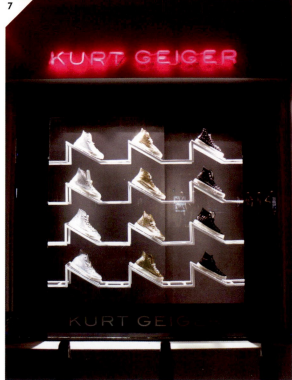

6
7

Arcade window

These windows are set back from pavement view, so the viewer has to walk inside the arcade. There may be more emphasis on dressing side views as footfall is directional. Historically these types of store are small and narrow, so the arcade windows will be dressed to display the store contents.

Fashion showcase / window boxes

Small display boxes do not cover the full height and width of the main fascia or store window; they may even be set aside from the retail space entirely. This format works very well for displaying smaller products, such as jewellery, and helps to draw the consumer's eye to small details and intriguing displays.

8

Windowless

Some retailers completely remove all window spaces to open up the full entrance space from the outside in. Such formats are often found in shopping malls or freestanding promotional spaces. The threshold space is immediate and can be used as a third window opportunity.

6 Arcade window and entrance,
  Old Bond Street, London.
7 Showcase display at Kurt Geiger.
8 Display cases at Ben Sherman.

Retail windows

Temporary backgrounds

There are countless ways to enclose a space temporarily: screens, hanging graphics, panels, suspended objects and curtains can all be used to change the dynamics of a window space.

Fashion windows in isolation

In some European and Asian countries it is possible to see outdoor-style windows in isolation from the main store. These form part of the journey to sale by confronting the shopper on the street. In this scenario, it is wise not to display expensive merchandise that is prone to theft and to consider how the shopper will view the scheme from 360 degrees.

Changing window displays

Floors

Traditional window spaces tend to feature removable flooring that needs to be covered or painted after every window scheme change. The flooring is an integral part of the window preparation and it is usually removed, recovered or painted in conjunction with the rest of the window area preparation. Floor base panels may be cut to sizes that are manageable to lift in and out of the window, but do not show too many seams from the outside.

Window lighting

Lighting is generally hidden just above the window height unless it is unique and part of the overall window scheme. During each window change, lighting should be switched off, removed carefully and the individual lamps cleaned before they are reinstalled. Side lighting is particularly useful for windows that are high but shallow. Directional spot lighting is useful to highlight a particular focal point in the window.

9   An unusual, 'framed' window
display at Prada.

Retail windows

Window composition

It is quite common for customers to view a window scheme during installation so it is particularly important that every viewpoint is scrutinised in detail. When a potential customer passes by the window, particularly at a small independent store, they will hopefully look towards the newly installed scheme but perhaps also slightly beyond, so it is therefore essential to grab their attention by the time they reach the central point of the scheme. Larger retailers and department stores have the advantage of multiple windows, which manages this problem, but with smaller retailers it is important to consider the way the product is facing and to ensure that it is angled in the direction of the footfall or customer flow. Customers rarely approach a retailer face-on unless it happens to be situated opposite a designated road crossing, for example.

10

10 Window displays at Burberry, Zara and Topshop.

Removing an existing window scheme

The window space is crucial for generating sales so it is in the interest of the retailer that these spaces are empty for the shortest possible time between promotions. Retailers will often use graphic images to disguise the installation of a new scheme behind and the installations are usually built at night. After the removal of an existing scheme, some elements may be stored and recycled for future use. Once a scheme has been removed certain checks need to take place before the next scheme is installed:

× Merchandise removed from mannequins or placed in a window needs to be returned to the original departments. Fashion merchandise in particular needs to be security tagged and any kimbles or other tickets need to be reattached.
× Flooring should be removed, if necessary, before it is recovered in a new material or painted.
× Window lamps should be checked, cleaned and replaced as necessary (this is also essential as part of general maintenance).
× Electrical points should be checked.
× Existing full-backed window spaces are ordinarily repainted although may require some prior preparation such as filling of holes.
× Windows should be cleaned by a hired professional.
× Threads, staples or nails need to be removed.

Installing a window scheme

It is particularly important that adequate preparation time is given to the installation of a new scheme and careful planning prevents or at least manages potential delays. The following points should be considered as part of the preparation:

× When is the change planned?
× Has the scheme been designed?
× Are there particular promotions that need to be considered?
× Are there external consultants installing the scheme?
× Does the installation require particular types of merchandise?
× Is the merchandise currently available and in adequate quantities?
× Are there mannequins / bust forms available on which to present the merchandise if required?
× Do the mannequins / bust forms need renovating or do new ones need to be bought?
× Are there any props that need to be sourced, made or purchased?
× Who will paint the interior, the in-store team or an external contractor?
× Is there a need for skilled trades: carpenter, electrician or vinyl installer?
× Is there a schedule of works to ensure that everyone is aware of the details?
× Are there visual merchandisers available or do they need to be brought in from other sites? Are any freelance visual merchandisers needed?
× Do materials need to be sourced, such a floor coverings or a particular type of paint?

Mannequins

Using and handling mannequins in commercial environments is a key skill for visual merchandisers. The selection of merchandise that mannequins will wear is usually decided at a head office level in larger corporate organisations. In smaller organisations, it is possible to take responsibility for selecting the merchandise, and this should be in line with promotional activities and seasonal trends.

Types of mannequin

Mannequins come in many human-like forms and historically of course have changed styles according to the latest fashion trends. The majority of mannequins are now made of fibreglass, which is not particularly sustainable, so research is being undertaken by a variety of companies around the globe into production of mannequins in a variety of materials.

The figures themselves have usually been modelled from one or more men or women but they do not tend to be anatomically 'correct'. Rather, they are moulded to form an aspirational image of how we could appear if we were younger, slimmer and taller. Ultimately, the purpose of a mannequin is to sell products, so they must show merchandise at its best, and communicate the latest trends in fashion.

Styles of mannequins change according to need and should be selected to work with the particular brand values of the company. For example if a brand with an industrial 'look' were to select realistic and glamorous mannequins with wigs and detailed make-up it may contradict with the type of brand they are, instead they may favour a far more generic or vintage feel to their show their collections to their best advantage.

The range of availability of types is quite phenomenal and many companies have an extensive archive from which to draw on. The final finishes and body shapes can also be adjusted or developed according to the range of merchandise being sold. We have grouped the various types that we have identified as below:

11

12

Unrepresented figures

While most mannequin suppliers have whole ranges of figures to choose from, the majority used by retailers tend to be of the Caucasian variety. Figures reflecting Black and Asian ethnicities are produced by mannequin companies, but these are not always readily seen on the high street.

Abstract

Retailers who want to project a quite generic figure through their use of mannequins often opt for a mannequin which is presented facially in an abstract way. Abstract mannequins were used quite extensively throughout the 1980's in retail but gradually fell out of fashion although they are gradually becoming used more as pieces of art or to lead in differentiation.

Abstract product

Mannequins that are not actually used to present clothing but covered in perhaps smaller products such as multiples of props or food, for example, are referred to as abstract product mannequins. They are still mannequins but are used creatively to illustrate a retailer's product range in an unusual and exciting way.

Futuristic

Futuristic mannequins tend to have a 'space age' or metallic feel to them. Fibreglass can easily be chromed in a variety of colours in order to achieve this effect.

Fashion future

Fashion future collections are the ranges of mannequins that capture the essence of the here and now and are usually based on real celebrities or personalities who encapsulate the zeitgeist of the moment. These figures are usually a full-bodied mannequin sprayed in a natural skin tone with handmade wigs and make-up and designed to have a realistic image of the person that they have been modelled from.

11 Smythson mannequin body parts.
12 Universal Display.

Mannequins

Male mannequins
Male mannequins tend to be produced with the stereotypical male physique in mind. Some figures can be fairly muscular and therefore some products do not work well with them, particularly men's formal suits. Some figures can also either appear either Neanderthal or effeminate so the best solution is always to use figures that are simply formed and designed.

Headless/faceless
Mannequins do not always need to have a realistic head with fully recognisable features and heads can be removed at the manufacturing stage or a more generic mould of a head and added to simply give an impression rather than appear realistic.

Bust forms
Depending on the fashion brand, many retailers opt for bust forms rather than a full bodied mannequin which may fit particularly well with the type of brand they are. Bust forms are cheaper than mannequins and with the option of articulated arms and hands these are a very versatile 'vehicle' to show product from.

13 Patina-V mannequin by Cofrad.
14 Rootstein collection.
15 Joan Collins, alongside Rootstein's mannequins in the 1980s.

15

Child mannequins

Child mannequins generally follow the same design and manufacturing process as an adult figure although the amount of variety of these figures is quite limited.

Illusory mannequins

On occasions fashion retailers may not use any mannequins at all. The merchandise itself is prepared and presented as if a person was wearing it creating the illusion of a figure or 'invisible man' scenario.

Hybridised mannequins

A hybridised mannequin is a mannequin that has been placed in the wrong position or deliberately in a position in which it was not intended to be. While this is not always a terrible visual merchandising offence, it does make mannequins look quite odd.

Decorative mannequins and bust forms

As with 'abstract product' mannequins decorative mannequins and bust forms are often used purely as props. Figures can be painted, covered in materials such as mosaics or vinyl and support the overall theme of an installation.

Collections

Each year, mannequin suppliers offer their latest collections (some twice a year) for purchase. These collections are normally presented within showroom spaces owned by the supplier and follow a theme based on trends in colours, in styles, body shapes and sizes.

Ten considerations when selecting mannequins for your visual concept

What is your budget? Mannequins can cost up to £1000 ($1500) per piece.

× What is your concept? Are the mannequins appropriate to your brand?
× What is the lead time? How long will it take to get to receive the mannequins?
× Will they stand alone or will they be grouped together?
× Where will you find inspiration for Wigs, make-up and body colours?
× Who will dress your new and expensive figures when they arrive? How will you communicate your inspiration to the supplier?
× Are these people experienced in handling mannequins or do they need training?
× Who will organise maintenance of your mannequins and organise for them to be updated when necessary?
× Will you wire or use glass base plates? Consider the floor type, for example, will the mannequins stand on marble/ wood/ glass?
× How long is your investment going to last? A customer will rarely notice that the merchandise has been perfectly prepared but certainly will notice if it has not been.

Selection of fashion merchandise

The selection of fashion merchandise for promotion is often a collaborative process between departments, with creative directors detailing promotion information in advance. This could include seasonal, publicity or special promotional activities that need to feature concurrently with advertising. Particular features of the merchandise can be noted and highlighted within an installation. Any accessories such as shoes, jewellery and so on, will also be selected to build on the narrative.

Product grouping

Groupings communicate brand values and reflect the retailer's corporate strategy. The following visual merchandising techniques are commonly used:

Commodity grouping
The grouping of one type or style of product in a range of colours. Retailers such as Gap and Uniqlo use this technique to create a critical mass of product offer.

VISUAL MERCHANDISING SPACE SELLING STRATEGIES

Accessories

Jersey separates

Shoes

Front print T-shirts

Outerware

Denim storey

Check shirts

Button front hooded tops

Casual cotton trousers

Best-selling chunky knits

Customer entrance and directional movement around store

16 Product adjacency wheels demonstrate the ideal product positioning and logical adjacencies. The customer flow, entrances and exits, price hierarchy, product purpose, product end use and brand positioning all play a major part in creating the customer journey. An adjacency wheel can be used to achieve product presentation consistency over multiple stores.

16

Coordinated ranges

The display of products within the original ranges they were designed and bought for.

Wardrobing

The mix of core lines or everyday items with high fashion products to achieve different looks. This technique works well to build a wardrobe range customers may have at home, encouraging them to mix and match product options from a wider selection.

Trend-led

The presentation of products that reflect current trends.

Outfit building

Presentation of head-to-toe solutions to suggest exactly what the customer should buy and wear together.

Women's fashion

It is particularly important to be aware of the key trends when selecting women's fashion items. Good communication with buyers, merchandisers, marketing and PR departments is critical, as is reading the latest fashion magazines, newspaper articles, blogs, watching fashion media and, wherever possible, attending fashion week shows. Knowledge of fashion itself cannot be underestimated, and this should include an international fashion perspective.

High-quality fashion products usually require little preparation although steaming and/or ironing where appropriate is crucial. A well-manufactured garment should not need much pinning on the mannequin, but should it be required it must be discreet and out of view. Mannequins should be grouped and positioned towards the main footfall. Mannequins that have the ability to be placed in multiple positions make the job a little easier but should never distort the product itself.

17 Merchandise on display
    at Splash store, Dubai.

17

Selection of fashion merchandise

ACCESSORIES ON G

18

Fashion accessories

Accessories must be appropriate and complement the overall look. It is worth remembering that most mannequin hands do not move and attempting to attach a handbag or umbrella, for example, will destroy the overall appeal. Mannequins with articulated hands are limited in their availability and may not be appropriate to the brand image. Expensive jewellery is usually shown within an enclosed, secure environment.

The best quality handbags are usually selected as part of a current trend or promotion. It is important to remember that the outside face of the merchandise should be shown, as this is how it would be carried or worn.

Lingerie and hosiery

Lingerie is usually presented in a sensual way that highlights fabrics and seasonal or fashionable colours. Specialist lingerie departments and stores are often designed to create an intimate, gentle atmosphere with emphasis on feminine qualities. Life-sized mannequins or bust forms are generally used in a smooth finish. Textured or covered figures should always be avoided.

Stockings and tights are usually displayed on leg forms and used in a repetition format to show the variety of available tones and designs. There are of course opportunities to explore different, more exciting ways to display this kind of product.

Headwear

Hats are not as extensively worn today as they were in the past, and are usually reserved for special events such as weddings or the races. Fixtures for this type of product do not vary extensively, and head forms are generally used. Sunglasses are often placed within high-density fixtures in repetitive rows, broken up with the use of mirrors and brand promotional material.

Shoes

There is less flexibility with shoes as they are essentially small product items. Preparing shoes for presentation is particularly important, as the customer will often scrutinise them in detail. Every item needs to be free from marks or defects and finishes such as suede need to be carefully brushed.

Women's footwear tends to be more varied than men's and can be divided generally into particular ranges, such as eveningwear, casual, fashion, work shoes and so on. The visual merchandising should take into account how these will be presented and the strongest solution is within its category of end use.

As with all fashion, shoe styles, colours, textures and materials change constantly and this should be considered as new products are launched and the key fashion elements are promoted.

18   Accessories on display at Liberty, London.
19   Louis Vuitton wooden shoe displays.
20   Men's footwear displays at Church's shoes, London.

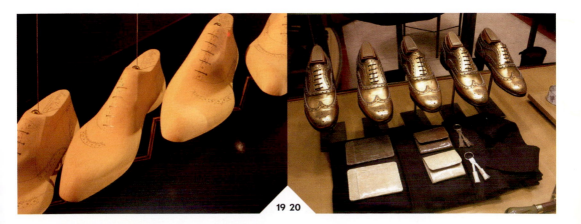

19 20

Selection of fashion merchandise

Menswear

Tailoring

It is particularly important to display tailoring as it would be worn. Full-bodied mannequins are generally used to show the product, and any details such as buttons or pockets, to their full potential. Men's mannequins tend to have a 38-inch chest and 30-inch waist and stand around 6 feet tall. The mannequin should be carefully selected: some figures have muscular arms and chests, which can make formal wear look out of shape. Trousers are nearly always shown in conjunction with men's jackets.

Shirts

The majority of men's shirts are visually merchandised using high-density fixtures and supported with the use of bust forms. Fortunately, there are a wide variety of forms on the market; those with articulated arms and hands work well, adding movement and interest to what can otherwise appear to be a fairly unexciting installation. Men's shirts vary in their cut and style and there may be particular details, such as cufflinks or a brand logo, which can be featured as part of the installation.

Underwear and socks

Men's underwear, including t-shirts, are best shown through the use of full torsos or lower torso forms sat in or on top of fixtures. Socks are often visually merchandised through the use of foot forms in a repetition format to communicate availability in a variety of colours.

Formal ties

As with all fashion merchandise the best way to show ties is as they would be worn, i.e. in a knot and merchandised with formal shirts with collars. In promotional terms it is always a good idea to keep in mind special events, such as weddings, or appeal to the target market where formal wear is a necessary part of working life.

21 Mixing men's and women's
shirts on display.

Selection of fashion merchandise

Shoes

As with women's shoes, it is good practice to prepare shoes for presentation, polishing if necessary, to show the product to its best advantage. The shoes should be laced appropriately, with laces untwisted and tied neatly or tucked inside. The instep of shoes is generally placed away from the customer view, with only the exterior shown. Men's shoes do not generally have enormous variation in colour, style and texture and can appear monotonous en masse. It is worth considering how this product can be made more interesting with the use of seasonal or promotional props and graphics.

Sportswear

Sportswear tends be light, colourful and often heavily branded or linked to a specific sports personality or event. Sportswear is also often displayed to highlight particular properties such as its ability to maintain body temperature, anti-slip properties or recycled fibres. Some brands offer customisation options such as personal identifiers and colour variations.

Children's wear

The principles for adult fashion merchandise equally apply to the selection and preparation of children's wear. Back-to-school promotions, which start in summer in the UK, are one of the main seasonal events. It can be a challenge to present this sort of merchandise, which tends to be dark tones, in an interesting and exciting way. Beyond the necessary school uniforms, children's wear needs to offer child as well as parent appeal and the use of fantasy and excitement is often critical in selling these types of products.

Preparation of merchandise

- Merchandise is identified and booked out from the stockroom or the shop floor.
- The removal of electronic tags, stickers, swing tickets and kimbles is important; these can easily be reattached once the scheme is dismantled.
- If the merchandise is an item of clothing, then the appropriate size for a mannequin or bust form should be selected. Depending on the brand, most ranges of mannequins are produced between a UK size 8 and 10 or 14 for a larger figure.
- Depending on quality and cost the merchandise is then either ironed or steamed. Luxury fashion items should always be steamed to remove any creases from packaging and transportation. Less expensive merchandise that creases easily may require both steaming and ironing, although care should be taken with a very hot iron and it is important to check the fabric and care labels.
- Packaged merchandise can be used although the packaging itself should be in perfect condition.
- Perishable goods are not usually placed within window schemes when a synthetic alternative can be used.
- Some merchandise may also need brushing, dusting or polishing and this can easily be done with the use of a clean cloth or sticky tape.
- Merchandise that has cracks, chips, tears or is damaged in any way should never be selected.

22   Display of men's formal footwear at Foster & Son.

Landscaping

Landscaping is used to create a space hierarchy within a store by recreating the height order of a natural landscape, graduating from the lowest to the highest point. The customer's view point leads from the fixtures at the end of the threshold, which should be lowest in height, such as tables (lakes), then built up on to feature or capacity fixtures (trees), which in turn lead the eye on to the merchandised back wall area with bulk or large capacity fixtures (mountains). This arrangement provides the best possible view of merchandise and store displays as the customer walks through the decompression zone.

Landscaping is used in theatre productions through stage design. A store window or interior space can be approached in a similar way, with the visual experience developing in different areas, created by controlled combinations of fixtures, colour, merchandise, lighting, props, graphics and surface material changes. Landscaping encourages customers to shop from the front to the back of the store, so fashion product should ideally be merchandised from floor to wall, rather than perimeter and floor separately.

22

VM SELLING STRATEGIES: LANDSCAPING THE RETAIL ENVIRONMENT

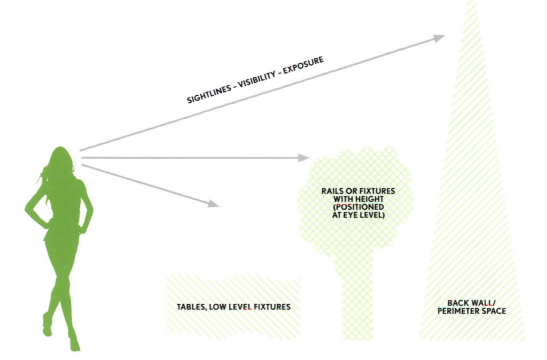

SIGHTLINES – VISIBILITY – EXPOSURE

RAILS OR FIXTURES WITH HEIGHT (POSITIONED AT EYE LEVEL)

TABLES, LOW LEVEL FIXTURES

BACK WALL/ PERIMETER SPACE

22 Landscaping in action at a Gap store in London.
23 Visual merchandising strategies: Landscaping the environment.

Fixtures

Successful visual merchandising takes into account levels and accessibility to customers in order to create a 'see it, like it, buy it' scenario. A basic table fixture for instance, which is good for heavy merchandise or bulky materials such as denim and jumpers, can be viewed at waist level and the merchandise is within easy reach for customers to touch and feel; this is a particularly important part of the customer experience and therefore leads to sales. Items displayed at a high eye level in store are more likely to gain exposure as the end of a long sightline. However, smaller items placed at high or low levels are lost, and larger or more bulky items work better at lower levels.

Selecting fixtures

When considering the types of fixtures that a retail spaces requires, it is particularly important to consider the following points:

× From what type of fixture do customers buy the most products?
× Which fixtures offer maximum exposure to the customer?
× From which position within a fixture do customers buy the most products?
× How is the fixture going to work in the space?
× Is the fixture material appropriate to the type of brand?
× Is the fixture in an appropriate material for its job?
× What are the visual merchandising opportunities that can be gained from using a specific type of fixture?
× How much merchandise does a particular fixture hold?

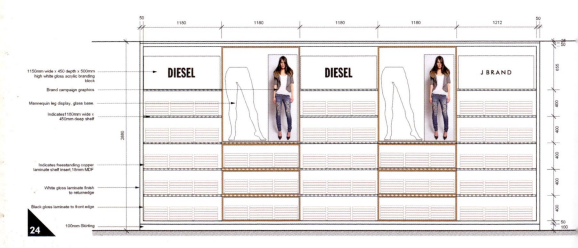

To ensure the product is enticing and 'easy to shop', the fixture must be effective, well maintained and appropriately supported with key visual merchandising elements. Retail store fixtures tend to be a long-term, expensive investment, so design and choice should be appropriate for the type and density of product/brand. Selected fixtures must perform efficiently and effectively for as long as possible, so factors such as appropriateness, functionality, materials and style will be taken into account.

A well-organised layout of fixtures within a store design, whether it is an exhibition, loop or race-track format, will help to create an effective selling space. The fixtures should allow the customer to flow freely through the store and not block sightlines, focal points or create physical barriers. Because of this, fixtures often work best at differing heights.

24 Repetition and balance within a denim merchandising wall unit.
25 Eye-catching displays at Marks & Spencer.

25

Fixtures

Types of fixture

Bulk / large capacity product fixtures

Bulk or large capacity fixtures, as the name suggests, carry large amounts of merchandise within the retail space. Because of their size, these types of fixtures tend to be used at the back of the store to carry merchandise such as denim, shoes and trainers.

Metal fixtures

Conventional metal fixtures are the staple choice for most retailers. Brushed steel is the most popular finish today, compared to a few years ago when one would find many examples of a highly chromed, mirror-like finish in retail stores. Metal fixtures are produced as round rails in various formats, four-way fixtures and t-stands. All have adjustable height mechanisms to accommodate the varieties in length of fashion products throughout the year.

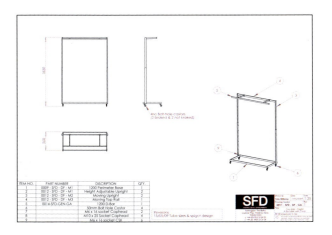

26 Design specification sheets for hanging rails by SFD (Shop Fitting Direct).

27 Design specification sheets for a table fixture by SFD.

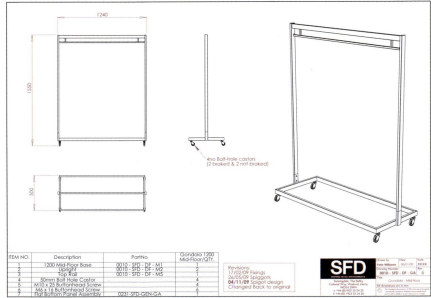

Gondolas

Gondolas are manufactured in a variety of materials; they act as a high/flexible capacity fixture, usually on wheels so they can be easily moved around a store. High-density merchandise, such as underwear, works particularly well on gondola fixtures, with opportunities to add images or shelves with bust forms and often storage underneath for easy stock replenishment.

Cubes

Cubes are used to carry large amounts of merchandise. These types of fixtures are most widely used for denim, enabling the merchandise to be folded and placed in order of size, cut and colour, which simplifies product selection for the customer.

Table fixtures

Tables are probably the most widely used fixtures in stores as they act as the 'lakes' within the landscaping techniques. These may be positioned just past the decompression zone to create opportunities for current promotions or around the retail space to break up the monotony of metal fixtures carrying bulk merchandise.

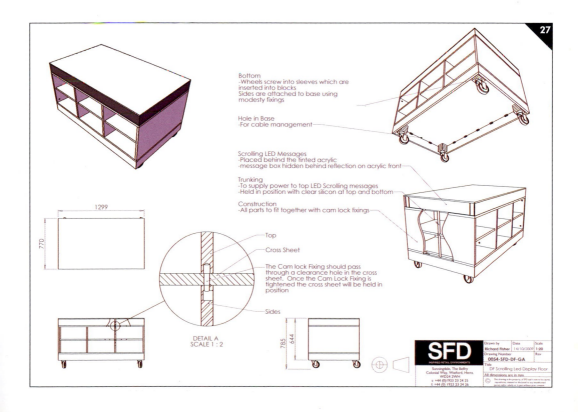

Fixtures

28

Feature fixtures
Fashion feature fixtures are normally designed to carry specialist or small amounts of merchandise that may be on promotion. These types of fixtures tend to be sprinkled around a commercial space and may contain items such as a pair of trousers, trainers, a variety of tops and perhaps a jacket, to go with the whole outfit.

Brand signature fixtures
With every high street brand vying for the customer demographic, differentiation is particularly important. The customer needs to recognise a brand and its signature of a particular space. Brand signature fixtures communicate such brand information and for this reason tend to be placed towards the front of the commercial space.

Antique furniture used as fixtures
In order to create some form of differentiation and add interest to the store environment, many retailers are now using different styles of antique or vintage furniture such as wardrobes, cabinets and tables as fixtures. Brands such as Anthropologie do this exceptionally well, even offering the fixtures themselves for sale.

28 Denim department fixtures by SFD for House of Fraser.
29 Spec sheet for perimeter wall design, by SFD.

Custom-made fixtures

Some brands move a step further and combine antique or vintage pieces to create specialised fixtures. This might include the use of elements such as old-fashioned suitcases and trunks strapped together to form a fixture or old tables joined together at oblique angles to form one piece.

Brand specific fixtures

Some brands supply specific fixtures for their products to be sold in store. Duty-free areas are probably the best example of this, with fixtures that may contain images of the product in the form of a large graphic, brand promotions, video screens or celebrity endorsements, perhaps with illumination to enable the product to stand out. Brand specific fixtures enable the manufacturer to control how the product is displayed and therefore retain brand image.

Perimeter grid walls and slat walls

Some retailers use grid walls and slat wall fixture systems along the perimeter space. Grid wall systems tend to be found in outdoor pursuits stores rather than fashion stores, although there are some that use these fixtures. Merchandise is hung on metal arms that hook on to the metal grid, offering a cheap and versatile system. Slat walls are a similar format, where the arms for the merchandise slot into grooves in the panels.

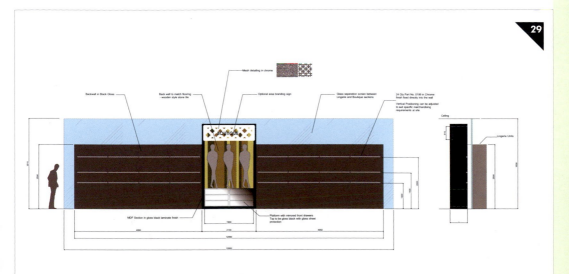

Area: Boutique

Case study: Harlequin Design

Overview

Harlequin Design is a London-based design agency specialising in brand development, retail, print, online marketing and PR solutions. Its core business is in fashion retail, operating on a global scale for clients from San Francisco to Shanghai. The design team implements cost-effective designs and visual merchandising projects at every level of the market. Harlequin Design generates concepts, produces design development visuals, installs visual merchandising schemes and manages windows displays to store graphics, websites; whatever a brand needs to build and maintain a strong and successful retail image.

In this case study we explore in depth one of Harlequin Design's clients, the men's fashion retailer Hackett.

HACKETT WINDOW DISPLAYS

Harlequin's scheme concepts for Hackett range from shirt-print butterflies to literary displays.

The project

The briefing process is developed with Hackett's creative team, who presents the vision and merchandise for the season using mood boards. The mood boards are categorised into the brand's various collections such as Mayfair, Brown in Town, Back to the Blues and so on. The designers have a good knowledge and understanding of the Hackett brand; its British heritage is a key part of the brand image and this is considered as part of the briefing process.

Case study: Harlequin Design

The design process

The design process involves the research of new ideas and concepts through to design development. The process begins with initial sketches of ideas made at one of the London-based stores, such as Sloane Street. Hackett's stores are orientated towards a local target audience and the Sloane Street store appeals to the wealthy businessman who may be looking for tailoring and suits. The nearby Regent Street store has a predominantly tourist footfall and presents a more casual offering, such as polo shirts and sweaters. The designs need to work across the different sites and appeal to a varied customer demographic.

A series of four to five designs are presented to the client, with some contingency concepts on the rare occasion that none of these designs is approved. Chosen concepts may then be mocked up in more detail in a store window.

The design team know the layout and dimensions of every store and can begin to identify and digitally communicate how the design will look in each location. These spaces are dramatically different: some may be situated within an historical space, others within shopping malls, so it is critical to have information about every site. The flagship stores in London, Madrid and Paris contain the whole brand concept, and versions are gradually filtered through to the smaller branches as well as the international stores. These stores will often receive a value engineered version of the scheme and implement it locally, so clear communication is crucial.

This scheme was based on Hitchcock's *The Birds*, using key imagery from the film such as the 'H' and the black crows. Development of the concept involved finding a way to tie the crows to the telephone wire without them falling over, and communicating this to stores for implementation.

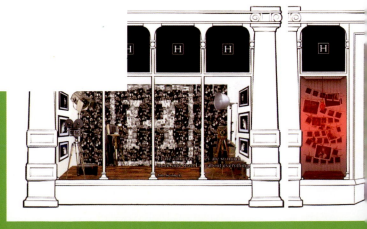

Installation

In some cases just one week is given to design, plan, manufacture and install a new scheme. This is increasingly becoming the norm, which means the design team has to organise the manufacture of certain props before the final sign-off stage.

The installation of schemes at the flagship stores involves a large team of workers, which enables them to troubleshoot any unforeseen issues. Representatives from the brand are also present, which helps them to understand the process and where necessary communicate this information to the smaller stores without teams.

CONCEPT COMPLETION AND INSTALLATION

Carrying out the design and manufacture of a scheme, often under tight deadlines, requires hard work from a vast team.

Case study: Proportion>London

Overview

Proportion>london is a design-led visual merchandising company specialising in the design and manufacture of mannequins, bust forms and a wide variety of visual merchandising equipment. The company has a long heritage, having descended from Siegal and Stockman in 1867 and today it still manufactures papier-mâché bust forms and torsos for use by workrooms, couture house design studios and dressmakers' showrooms.

The development process

The body shape is one of the first considerations followed by the style of head. The first figure is usually the most difficult to produce and the longest in development and production. Often the straightest or simplest pose is selected for development first, but the team considers the collection holistically to ensure that the developing collection of mannequins will work cohesively.

If a live model is employed then poses are agreed with the client. There are always certain imperfections that need to be refined in order to produce an aspirational mannequin. The body model is often different from the head model. Working collaboratively with the client and sculptor, the team is able to suggest potential solutions using a specific face model or producing references from archive images.

Once the pose is agreed, the model is photographed from 360 degrees and all measurements are taken; there could be as many as 60 measurements in total. All of this information is recorded before the sculptor begins work.

PROPORTION STUDIO

Modelling, sculpting and building in progress at the Proportion studio.

The initial stage of sculpting involves building an armature, a metal 'skeleton', which is then loaded with clay and blocked in to form a basic figure.

The head is often 'sketched in' using a simple block of clay for an impression of the figure's final height. It is usually produced separately on a stand that slots easily into the neck of the torso.

The next stage of development is to fit clothes on the clay figure. These may include a jacket, a slim-fit shirt, a pair of tight jeans and underwear. Stock shoes are cut in a way that allows the insole to be slid beneath the clay foot. If all works well at this stage, then the figure is approved by the client.

Case study: Proportion>London

Manufacturing stage

The clay figure is cut into its composite limbs and plaster moulds are made. Fittings that attach the arms to the torso are inserted and the plaster master figure is then assembled and finished; a process of meticulous sanding, filling and slight reshaping where small adjustments are needed.

Using a second set of clothes the plaster figure is dressed to test ease of use for the client. Particular attention is paid to the head, hands and legs, which are generally focused on when a mannequin is dressed in store.

The plaster figure is remoulded and produced in fibreglass form which can be moulded and stored as a master for subsequent production. The next stage is to check that all the technical aspects of the figure are correct, that it stands securely and upright and there are no health and safety issues. The figure is agreed before a final robust production grade mould is made. The whole process takes approximately three months.

Each mannequin part is manufactured from the moulds. A team of laminators produces a basic figure using a gel coat, resin and fibreglass matting. The resultant figure goes through two stages of finishing, which involves sanding and refining the features. The figure is then primed and painted.

Mannequin make up is applied using oil paints and requires a skilled artist. A fine nylon filament is used as hair, which is glued to a buckram base before cutting and styling to the client's requirements. Wigs are then lacquered and baked at a low temperature to set the style.

MANNEQUIN MANUFACTURE

Building and finishing the mannequins in the Proportion studio.

RESEARCH AND DESIGN

5

This chapter introduces the creative processes involved in developing new concepts for visual merchandising.
Although predominantly a creative discipline within retail, visual merchandising is very much commercial in its outcome.
Visual merchandising strategies should ultimately generate sales for the retailer by entertaining and enticing customers to buy.

Global visual branding still dominates the market with the more eccentric, theatrical schemes currently in the minority (these tend to be used by luxury brands, department stores and small boutiques) but much admired. It is important to tap into localised market places in order to reach the target market and differentiate the brand.
This chapter explores a variety of strategies to challenge the more conventional ways of interpreting visual merchandising ideas, supporting the brand, product and the environment in a creative way.

1   A theatrical window display at
    Harvey Nichols, London.

Visual design development

There are numerous ways to enhance creative thinking: reading publications, experiencing different cultures, surrounding oneself with other creative people, visiting shows, exhibitions and galleries and so on. As visual researchers we already do these things, but we can be more strategic with the creative processes. The following section outlines techniques that can be used as starting points to activate the creative thinking process.

Mind mapping

Mind mapping or mind storming are extremely useful in the development of concepts. Essentially it is an organic diagram on which we collect random words and visuals. By using Tony Buzan's method of Radiant Thinking, we can activate the brain's ability to generate creative ideas. The process begins initially with one word or a central image, which could be a theme or concept or something completely random, such as a feeling, colour or mood. The word will expand into other words by association with the addition of branches stemming from the main word/image.

2

2 Visual inspiration can be found virtually anywhere.

This process will naturally stop once you have established multiple points of interest to investigate. It ensures that visual merchandising designers have covered a wide range of ideas and that all potential sources have been identified and exploited as possible leads and concepts for design.

When we begin to develop new concepts, ideas, innovative ways of working, exciting ways of shopping, new experiences and visually merchandised environments, it is helpful to ask the following questions:

What is it?
A mood board / concept board, where the starting point is a randomly selected word.

Why are we doing it?
This is a useful process to begin generating new ideas and ways of thinking, to move forward and shape the future of our visual merchandising industry.

How are we going to get there?
We are going to research the meaning of our randomly selected word. The word can be placed at the centre of the board and we can unravel its meaning and build on a variety of new ideas and combinations of types of visual merchandising and ways of shopping.

Why do we need to generate new visual merchandising ideas? We have the power to create, improve and reshape our environment and lives through, for example, practical experimentation, skill development, knowledge and technology. Most of us live by working and by producing a product or service to others. Ultimately, we design new and exciting visual merchandising to survive the future and ensure longevity in our careers.

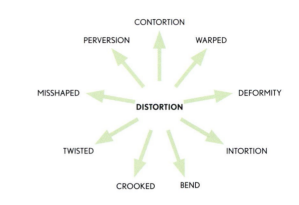

3

3   An example of a visual mind map.

Visual design development

4

Journey techniques

Documenting a journey can often lead to unexpected inspiration. In the example shown here, participants were asked to experiment in their approach to visual research methods by using disposable cameras. The participants had to resist the temptation of taking photographs of each other and focus more on abstract images found on their physical journey. Initially the group members were taken from Regent Street to Oxford Circus (the central shopping district in London). Participants began to navigate their way through the crowds and traffic while following signs and photographed anything of significance along the way. They were also given a list of significant words, such as energy, flexible, focus, texture, signage, graphics, metamorphosis, space and identity, to keep in mind while they recorded their images.

The quality of the images was by no means perfect but this was not important, the ideas and subjects recorded were far more pertinent. The journeys were recorded in 30 exposures or less.

These images tell a narrative of the individual perspectives and visual signposts that make up a journey. Each story is told and experienced differently, although everyone took the same route. This reflects the absolute nature of audience engagement and interpretation, which is an integral part of the visual merchandiser's role of adapting to multiple spaces by subjectively informing.

Lateral thinking

Lateral thinking promotes liberation from old ideas by always examining an alternative approach. It is very distinctive in breaking free from what is assumed. Vertical thinking is a more traditional approach, in which one moves forward a step at a time for each progression. Lateral thinking is more about seeking alternative information and solutions; challenging convention with no limitations on thought or ideas. Lateral and vertical thinking are complementary and can be exercised together.

Lateral thinking can be applied to many design situations but is particularly helpful in addressing specific design, display and innovation problems within visual merchandising. According to Edward De Bono, its main benefits are problem solving and new idea generation.

Scrapbooks

Scrapbooks are useful for gathering pieces of visual information and collaging them in new ways. Both sketchbooks and scrapbooks are personal and are not usually required in presentation for a client; but it is good practice to keep scrapbooks separate from sketchbooks and well organised to maintain clarity of thought.

They may include found or secondary images such as:
× Night club flyers
× Train tickets
× Bus tickets
× Photographs
× Invitations to events
× Exhibition flyers
× Postcards
× Magazine and newspaper articles
× Images that evoke a previous experience

Scrap book images should contain some notes as a reminder of where they were found; this information may be needed to reference future projects or simply to help locate them again if necessary.

5

4 + 5 Collaged images visually communicate the experience of two participants.

Visual design development

Sketchbooks

Sketchbooks are an essential visual record. It may be easier to capture and record image through digital means, but by drawing we become rather more critical of what we see. While digital images are of significant value, drawing is a skill that should be mastered at a level required to communicate one's intentions. Here are a few suggestions for elements to include in your sketchbook:

× Hand-sketched live drawings
× Critical analysis of researched visual information
× A record of mind mapping activities
× Sketches of concept development
× Sketch plans
× Space and zone plans
× Contextual studies
× Visual audits
× Testing and development of concepts
× Images of sketch models

Visual audits

Conducting a visual audit of a brand and its competitors helps to benchmark where we are, to reflect on what we are doing right and enable us to identify areas for future development. Visual merchandising can be a subjective part of the retail business, where people like to express their very personal likes and dislikes when selecting schemes. This can be counteracted by thoughtful and process-led analysis to back up ideas and proposals. The benefits of visual auditing include:

× Assess strengths and weaknesses
× Be the eyes of the customer
× Identify 'best practice' – cherry pick ideas
× Benchmark your business in the market
× Provide inspiration and spark new ideas
× Practise advanced observation skills
× Apply constructive criticism
× Understand and identify current trends in visual merchandising
× Support the development of new concepts
× Identify product presentation dynamics
× Establish the various components that make up a brand or shopping experience.

Visual merchandising is a collective term for everything visual within a store. Regular assessment of competitors during a 'competitive shop' encourages the creation of something above and beyond what has been created before, as well as keeping up to date with new concepts and ideas, especially when examining inspirational brands.

There are several approaches to creating a visual audit. Within most areas of the retail business, such as buying, merchandising and fashion product design, benchmarking exercises are conducted so as to keep a competitive edge. It is best to examine more than one store to gain perspective of the local market and expectation. Visual audits can also be used within the business to standardise visual merchandising principles and application. Areas for visual observation could be split into the physical zone areas or visual components of the store, such as windows, merchandise presentation, perimeter wall space, flooring, lighting, promotions, mannequins and props, ticketing, graphics, cash desk, fixtures, furniture, fittings and so on.

6   Pages from student Natalia
     Misiun's sketchbook.

Model making and experimentation

A model is a three-dimensional interpretation of a design, construction, idea, concept or intention. Working with a three-dimensional model enables a coherent exploration of the space and a visualisation of physical space and movement.

On completion of the early stages of visual research it is then appropriate to conduct further experimentation and practise 3D techniques. Viewing visual merchandising concepts from a three-dimensional approach is essential: only in-store graphics are viewed in two dimensions in a store context so it is imperative to build a realistic representation of an object, mannequin, prop or installation.

Types of model

Concept model
Concept models tend to be minimal and convey the idea or concept behind the visual merchandising scheme.

Sketch model
Sketch models are used to explore design aspects of a scheme and to present the design proposal in various stages of working progress.

Working model
These tend to be created for larger, long-term projects, such as architectural buildings.

Materials used for all types of model include:
× Plywood
× Poly (foam) board
× Paper
× Balsa wood
× Thin cardboard
× Plastic
× Acetate

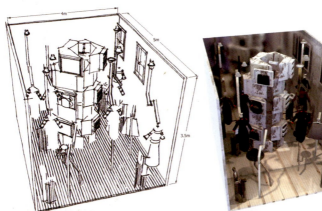

7   Sketches of visual merchandising schemes and digtial model interpretations.

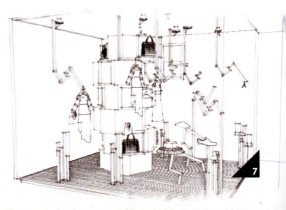

7

8 Models exploring shape
   and form.
9 Student Sasha Molyneaux's
   mini window concept model.
10 Student Qian Koh's mini
   window concept model.
11 Student Louise Kidger's mini
   window concept model.
12 Student Natalia Misiun's mini
   window concept model.

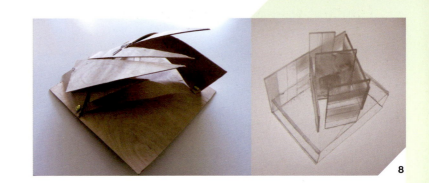

8

9 10

11 12

Concept development

Design ideas and concept development progressively lead on from the initial stages of visual research. Visual research exercises encourage visual merchandisers to look at the vast visual resources around them and to investigate primary resources rather than relying on the Internet or other secondary resources. This inspiration can be used as the basis for future projects and delivering informed solutions to design problems.

Surveying the space

It is important to survey a space, not only to consider the context in which the designs will be displayed, but also to identify opportunities, restrictions and limitations that may not be evident without a site visit.

The visual merchandiser must ensure that the designs will actually work with, and fit, the space. If this is not done correctly then the impressive graphic that has been designed or the large props that have been ordered may not fit, which wastes both the time and money of the client or company. It is therefore critical to understand and perform this process and to communicate it to others.

Floor plans, sections and elevations are often obtainable from the local public planning offices for a small fee, or they may be available from the architect. Most plan drawings dated pre-1970 in the UK will have been drawn in imperial measurements so it is important to also take accurate metric measurements, which is the conventional unit of measurement around the world (the exception is the USA, where imperial measurements are used).

Taking measurements

While there are high-tech solutions and digital measuring techniques available, being able to take measurements is a particularly useful technique to help you understand the spaces in which you will be working. It applies to any location around the world, and is an excellent, reliable skill to add to your portfolio.

Measuring will include interior spaces and windows. Some windows may be closed-back spaces, essentially a box with one side glazed as the store window, with access through a door at the back. Open-back window spaces are rather easier to work with, although it is still important to ensure that display items will fit.

Materials required:
× Pencil
× Eraser
× Ruler
× Paper
× Graph paper
× Scale ruler
× Tape measure (at least 18m long)
× Set square
× Scale ruler (typical scales are 1:100 for large spaces and 1:50 for smaller spaces)
× Compass

13 Image of a measured window space.

Familiarise yourself with the space before you begin, and confirm with the client exactly what space or spaces you will be working with. Roughly sketch the plan view of the space on a blank piece of paper. If you are unsure what a plan view would look like, imagine viewing the space from above without the ceiling, what would you see? Not all spaces have rooms with walls that meet at right angles and very often the space may contain structural elements, such as pillars or ramps, which must be included.

Begin by measuring across the space from corner to corner, and record on paper with dashed lines to indicate each measurement. If you are taking measurements alone it may be easier to lay the tape measure on the ground, if possible. At this stage ignore any temporary non-structural elements such as radiators, air conditioning units, light switches and so on.

Then take height and width measurements of walls, doors and windows; this is especially important where the ceiling is suspended overall or varies in height. Draw a rough outline drawing of each of the walls. Anything that needs to be placed within the space will have to pass through the doorway so it is essential to know the heights of these beforehand.

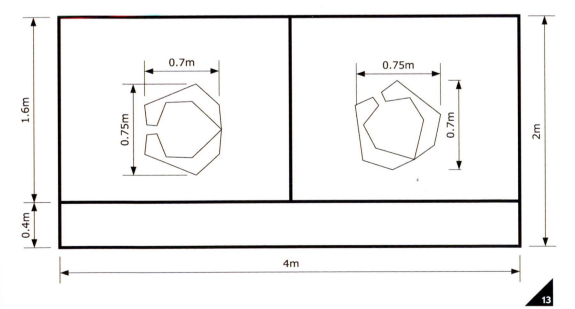

Concept development

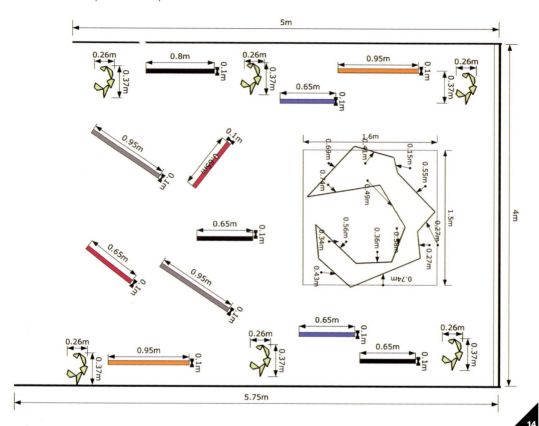

14

Transferring the plans onto graph paper

Once all of the measurements have been taken, they can be transferred in pencil onto graph paper at an appropriate scale for the size of the space. It is easiest to use one square on the graph paper to represent 1 square metre.

There is a simple technique for drawing pillars accurately. Measure the distances to and from the corners of the space, and then set your compass to zero and extend to this measurement equivalent on the scale ruler. Transfer the scale measurement to the graph paper by placing the compass at one point on the paper and making an arc. Several measurements can be scaled and drawn in this way until all four corners of the pillar are in place in the form of arcs. Draw the pillar by joining up the points where the arcs meet.

It is worth noting that you will nearly always have to re-measure some dimensions. Once the plan is completed, the elevations should be drawn in relation to the plan. This becomes the 'master plan' from which you will be able to begin space zoning and designing the commercial space.

If you do not have access to CAD software, this hand-drawn technique is a simple and effective, low-tech means of utilising the measurements. However, there are various CAD programs available, such as VectorWorks, Mockshop, AutoCAD and 3D Max, for a more professional finish, as shown in these examples.

14 A scaled shop floor plan.
15 Creating scale representations
       for a project at SFD.

Presentation and communication of design concepts

Presentation boards represent a visual merchandising interior scheme or concept with the aid of product images and samples. It is far easier to 'sell' a concept to a client through visuals than words alone. The following definitions explore how to segment ideas and highlight the different types of boards to communicate a concept.

Sample board

Sample boards show clients the type of surfaces, such as flooring, unit surfaces and wall finishes, that you are proposing to use. Samples should ideally be placed in hierarchical order, i.e. the floor finishes at the bottom of the board and any visual merchandising element that is to be suspended at the top of the board. Sample boards provide the opportunity to study real samples of materials before any final decision is made; therefore, it should be tactile in order for the viewer to experience the actual surface and properties of the material.

16 Sample board by Choi Ho Lai.
17 A sample mood wall.

16

17

Mood board

Mood boards are made up of inspirational images to create an evocative look. They are used with sketches and drawings, together with three-dimensional forms to communicate the design concept. They tend to be used at an earlier stage of a project to indicate the emotional and contextual aspects of a design concept.

Mood wall

This is the same as the mood board, but on a grander scale. It can form part of your working studio space and be adopted as a shared working practice by the whole visual team to contribute to, develop and discuss in detail.

Presentation and communication of design concepts

Colour board

These boards are used to present a colour scheme or abstract mood. Swatches of colour can be applied to the board to communicate the tone, hue and value as well as the combination of colours in a scheme.

There are many colour sources available for inspiration, with trend prediction companies dictating the colours of the year/season. When designing a visual merchandising scheme, it is important to be aware of the differences of colour codes, especially when producing graphics and wall colours.

The RAL colour system is a set of internationally recognised colour codes. Pantone ® colours are most commonly used, especially with a view to using graphics or type. Independent paint company codes are also commonly recognised.

Trend board

A trend board defines and predicts a look, theme or scheme, featuring samples or images for a definitive look for colour, texture and form. Fashion trends can be adopted from the streets or from the catwalks, but boards can feature anything on the pulse from music, product, colours, surfaces and materials to the way in which something is worn or the latest 'must have' craze.

Lifestyle board

This depicts a customer/brand look or lifestyle through product images and/or a mix of samples. This must be desirable, inspirational and relevant to the company marketing strategy. Lifestyle images can show demographics, geographic and psychographic elements as well as other inspirational brand values.

Presentation techniques

While you will have your own personal style of presentation, some direction is always useful:

× Visuals could be in the form of photographs, magazine cuttings and newspapers although these should always be good quality and carefully cut out.
× Place visuals so that they look clean, uncluttered and read well. Avoid using images that are too small.
× Sometimes clients just want straightforward information presented in straight lines or in a grid and in just one format.
× For interest, overlapping visuals can work well or try mounting them on foam board first and maybe laid over a larger image.
× Grouped samples work better than separated out.
× Place relevant samples next to their relating visuals, i.e., the fabric sample next to the sofa, wall coverings next to flooring and so on.
× If you have strong colours the board needs to be balanced, so that one area is not the focus and all the information can be read.
× Create interest using different images, shapes and forms; for example, curved lines next to straight lines and so on.
× Always make sure that cuttings and samples are neat, straight and well attached.
× Simple line drawings and sketches can add a creative touch.
× Title the project and the products if relevant. However, do not overload the board with too much written information.

18 Trend board looking
    at puppetry,
    by Magdalena Choluj.

25 visual themes

Many visual merchandising schemes follow a theme. We have identified just a few here but they should serve to give you plenty of inspiration for your own research!

Theatrical

Theatrical schemes are a fantasy world in which 'larger than life' characters and settings exist; they are imaginative, dreamlike and generate the feeling of escapism. The creation of dramatic effects and storytelling are common themes within theatrical settings, which are often heavily propped, accessorised and dressed like stage sets.

Theatrical schemes entertain, attract and entice an audience. The use of props is prolific in theatrical window designs. Specialist props are often commissioned and made by prop makers and used in conjunction with simple items such as blocks and plinths that can be used several times. It is difficult to use anything unusual more than once, as it will be recognised by customers.

20

Conceptual

Conceptual schemes are based on design, art forms, movements or genres and, as such, often contain very little product. The emphasis here is on a way of thinking and communicating a message through creativity and imagination. The relationship between the product and brand may not always be obvious, although unconventional, challenging and inspiring design ideas should engage the mind of the customer.

Concept-led schemes are often developed in collaboration with artists, designers, museums, galleries or current exhibitions. Conceptual schemes challenge the customer's perceptions, making them stop and engage with the installation. They may contain sculptural props, works of art, embroideries and so on, shifting the focus away from the product being sold in store and more on the installation itself. Liberty in London will often challenge the conventions of window design, forming collaborations with the art, design and media industries or linking with current exhibitions; as a consequence, the balance between product and props is often challenged.

19 Bergdorf Goodman,
New York.
20 Liberty London.

25 visual themes

 21

Seasonal

Seasonal installations highlight key celebrations and events in the retail calendar. Community significant dates may be emphasised at a local level, as well as the more obvious seasonal displays for Christmas, Easter and spring/summer collections. Seasonal sale dates are set in the marketing calendar and vary little from year to year, in keeping with anniversaries, the weather and religious celebrations. Events are structured around meaningful dates in the consumer calendar and celebrated in stores to promote relevant products.

Lifestyle

Lifestyle schemes often use a mixture of props, materials and accessories to enhance the product, mood or atmosphere of an installation. A lifestyle installation scheme echoes the very nature of what we desire and want to buy into as consumers. A visually stimulating environment or realistic room set attracts the aspirational shopper who can easily translate the projected look to their own homes. Exciting, desirable and complementary lifestyle installations are versatile and can feature a number of products together with installation anchors to achieve visual impact. Lifestyle schemes are often used by homeware brands, which present a whole scene or scenario as if one could step inside and live in the space as it is.

22

23

Trends

Installations based on foundations such as social, economic, diverse or mainstream trends can tap into the mindset of the buyer to build a sense of understanding and belief; this in turn develops a stronger bond with consumer and brand. In terms of fashion trends, an installation could be based on a 'must have' or specialist product, communicating how to wear the trend or build the outfit. Trends that emerge from the street are just as significant as the catwalk; to the most fashion conscious brands it's all about the look being on-trend.

21   Tommy Hilfiger
     Juicy Couture Lifestyle
     Tods, Bond Street, London.
22   Ralph Lauren Kids
     Smythson
     Fat Face, London.
23   Prada Penhaligon's.

Nostalgic themes, sometimes depicted with humour or romance through theatrical window installations, evoke feelings of the past. A 'make do and mend' attitude (a necessity in the 1940s) has recently sparked a trend on the UK high street. It represents the consumer's mindset in an over-consuming society: people are strongly passionate about the notion of recycling and reuse, and stores have been getting creative with visual merchandising in response to this social trend.

25 visual themes

24 Maison Martin Margiela
   for Selfridges.
25 Selfridges.
26 Marc Jacobs political
   bull windows.
27 Diesel.

24

Colour

Schemes are often designed around a colour palette that could be based on the brand colour, a product, season, theme, promotion or campaign. Often the visual merchandising window concept will be developed as a general theme from which a group of colours can be derived to create an atmosphere. The use of just one colour can create a strong impact, such as the all-white Maison Martin Margiela scheme shown here. Using different colour combinations can have an emotional and behavioural effect on the viewer: some colours have calming properties whilst other hues can be energising and intense.

Heritage

Patriotic displays relate to a consumer's sense of belonging and association with a certain group. For example, over recent years the UK has celebrated a Royal wedding, Queen Elizabeth's Diamond Jubilee and hosted the Olympic games. British retailers used these special national occasions to boost retail sales, at the same time honouring British heritage. What was so interesting was the different ways in which retailers interpreted the same visual merchandising theme to create a variety of visual spectacles around the UK.

26

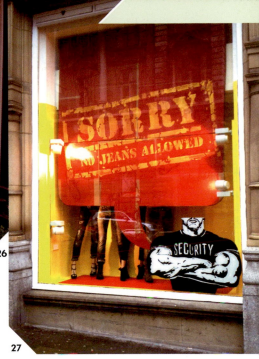

27

Political/parody

The socio-political climate doesn't always have an effect on window installations, but as communication advances and informs the international market, so the promotional angle of installations uses visual impact to inform, shock, challenge and commiserate. Visual merchandising can be used to make political statements or reflect current issues, although it takes a strong brand to make such public statements (and not many really do); however, most brands avoid contentious installations.

More commonly, the business of fashion can be seen to parody itself, with frivolous and highly emotive schemes used to intentionally cause a stir among viewers. Marc Jacobs's window installation, for example, signified the downturn of the New York stock exchange and we saw how this economic situation dramatically affected fashion spending, while consumers tightened their belts and braved the recession in early 2009.

Promotional

Price-led schemes are commercially important to any business. Using price points to promote a product in a store window is the most direct and literal technique. The combination of marketing campaign, collaboration with external industries, and a strong visually merchandised scheme can be used to create hype around a brand or product. Promotional strategies reinforce the 'journey to sale', as well as the image and identity of the brand.

The most common promotional activities include new product launches, such as perfumes or new collections, live windows (using people in windows to generate interest and excitement), media windows (using screens or projectors with clips of runway shows) and celebrity advertising campaigns with large photographic imagery.

25 visual themes

Graphics

The use of graphic images and text is undoubtedly one of the most cost-effective and low maintenance types of scheme. These are a useful form of communication, especially when viewed from afar, as a graphic can be blown out of proportion to create visual impact and attract extensive footfall. Graphics printed on different materials and objects can be implemented within the window space and window vinyl or decals can be used in conjunction with any type of scheme. A brand logo or symbol is commonly communicated through graphic display. Large or outsized props are often used to reinforce a message that may support the qualities of a particular product or simply be used to highlight a current promotion or seasonal event.

28

29

30

28 Kurt Geiger.
29 Converse.
30 Adidas.
31 Anya Hindmarch for
    Selfridges.
32 Belstaff.

31

Animatronics and animation

With the move towards ever-more sophisticated digital media, the days of animatronics and animation seem sadly numbered. The use of electrical motors to create turntables, oscillations and indexing (stopping and starting movements) has been relegated to the windows of just a few traditional brands around the world. Mechanical animated displays are very much alive in visual merchandising and a mixture of digital and mechanical craft is a popular approach to animated schemes.

32

25 visual themes

Digital media

Digital technology is an increasingly popular form of media in the retail environment. Digital displays range from projections, computer and TV screens, virtual and 3D hardware – all used to display product image and information in virtual or augmented reality (see also chapter 6). Digital media explores transformative and innovative techniques on the shop floor while engaging the customer with the product. Digital technology is increasingly sophisticated, with large video screens projecting the brand's latest catwalk collections and interactive technology with which we can photograph ourselves and e-mail the results to friends. It should be remembered, however, that the media itself is changing and updating constantly, and retailers need to keep up.

33

Humour-led

The things we find amusing are culturally linked, and what one culture may find amusing can offend another, so the visual merchandiser must be aware of this and work accordingly. In the UK, humour is often used as a key factor in defining a brand. Dry wit, funny scenarios and poking fun at stereotypes are entertaining and engage the customer as they pass by the windows. Humorous window schemes can provoke positive reactions and discussions, often with the use of the simplest of props or by manipulating the body language or look of mannequins.

Sex

Provocative schemes can cause a negative reaction in viewers but they will also attract attention and publicity if the retailer is prepared to defend such schemes. The retailer needs to determine how far they are prepared to provoke reactions but generally a non-explicit sex theme can be used to sell, tease and generally promote a fun attitude. Sensitivity to cultural surroundings naturally needs to be taken into account; some cultures will find these kinds of schemes offensive.

33 Barneys, New York.
34 Selfridges.
35 Agent Provocateur.
36 Victoria's Secret.

25 visual themes

37

Fashion

The monolithic emporiums that sell fashion-forward brands, such as department stores or a 'house of brands', are predominantly aimed at the fashion conscious customer who enjoys wearing the latest catwalk trends. This is usually reflected in the marketing campaigns and advertising through to the shop floor and store windows, closing the loop on the customer journey. These window designs reflect high fashion, the current top designer brands as well as shopping theatre, escapism and excitement. The clothing featured in the windows is often an exaggerated form of the outfits that are worn every day, designed to entertain the consumer and create a point of difference. As a visual merchandiser it is important to evaluate and categorise the different market levels within fashion retail so the product can be presented according to market sector. In essence, fashion-based window displays can emphasise a specific designer collection, a fashion trend or a key look for the season.

38

Product-led

Product-led schemes tend to be used by brands that are synonymous with a certain product, from which a whole scheme or narrative will be developed and designed. Consider Nike, for example: as well as its 'winning team' mantra, Nike is renowned for celebrating the integrity of its products through window displays. For such large window spaces the product always takes centre stage, and the message is big, bold and committed. The customer is convinced by the superpowers of the product because the brand has established itself as a leader in the field of sports merchandise.

39

40

Design

It is difficult to define contemporary design as it is constantly changing and moving. Schemes often use references to design in windows, ranging from historical movements and genres to particular products. Design (both good and bad) is a result of personal expression and it is open to interpretation. The key element here is to stress the differentiation of the brand and this can be achieved through design.

Text

The art of typography (the design of font and type) is seeing an upsurge in the world of design. In a visual merchandising context, typography can be used to provide information and/or feature as part of the decoration and backdrops. Typographical props come in all guises and can add a three-dimensional element to a scheme. As we have seen, text can be used on all sorts of surfaces and planes of space. The use of illustrative text, in particular, is commonplace in its application to props. Using props can challenge the focus of a display: not only do they make up the structure and composition, they can also be the primary focus within a more unconventional installation, which in some cases may not even feature any product.

41

37 A product led scheme at Gap, London.
38 Fashion product led scheme at McQueen, London.
39 Harvey Nichols.
40 Nourison, New York.
41 Helmut Lang, New York.

25 visual themes

Vintage and antique

The increase in online shopping and the phenomenal global success of sites such as eBay has contributed to a significant decline in bricks-and-mortar stores selling vintage and antique clothing. There are some retailers fighting back, offering the experience of touch and feel; markets in particular are fantastic places to find bargains, if one is willing to rummage. Many retailers also source props at such markets, which are also excellent places to identify forthcoming trends. Antique or vintage props are often used to add an unusual or surprise element to a scheme.

Lighting

Lighting can be used as the focus of a scheme. Some brands use illuminated lightboxes as installations in windows and in store. Brand logos or simply an indication of what is in store can be communicated through the window. It is worth noting that these types of installations, particularly with neon in enclosed spaces, may have health and safety implications in some countries and it is worthwhile seeking advice before commissioning anything to be made.

Narrative

Narratives are a form of storytelling. A narrative is best told through a sequence of windows, allowing a break between each chapter of the story. The Christmas 2012 windows of Lord and Taylor, in New York, are a perfect example of storytelling; the theme was based on an imaginary miniature world, depicting magical winter scenes. The scene in each window followed another, captivating viewers as if they were reading a book.

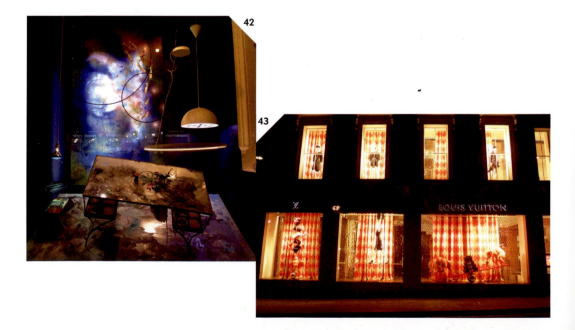

42

43

44

Sale

Sale or clearance is an inevitable period within the retail calendar: it occurs significantly at least twice a year and in smaller promotions throughout the year. Red has historically been the colour associated with a sale promotion; these days, however, stores are stretching visual merchandising concepts far beyond hanging red banners in the store windows. They are challenging the usual red-and-white sale graphic formats to entice a new, younger audience, as shown in the example here.

45
46

42   ABC, New York.
43   Louis Vuitton, London.
44   Calvin Klein, London.
45   Desigual, London.
46   Esprit, London.

25 visual themes

47

48

FOREST DAY OCTOBER 20, 2011
SAVE THE BRAZILIAN FOREST

Sustainability

Certain retailers have a sustainable strand
running through their brand profile and
product offer, which is translated to the
shop floor to project the ethos and nature of
the brand. Sustainable themes in windows
still remain uncommon, however, although
a good example is Selfridges' Ocean
Project, which sought to inform and educate
customers about sustainable fish farming in
a humorous way.

Charity

Charity associations with fashion brands
are becoming increasingly common, with
retailers linking up with charities to raise
money and raise brand profile. One example
is the 'Aqua for Life Project', formed by
Giorgio Armani's Acqua Di Gioia in
association with Green Cross International,
to raise awareness and funds to provide
clean water for children. L'Oreal briefed
Elemental Design to design and produce
promotional sites and a window display
at Harrods. They produced a scheme that
used a combination of textured Perspex and
lighting in panels, against clean, gloss white
fixtures to create a watery effect.

47 Anthropologie, London.
48 Anne Fontaine, London.
49 Gant store, London.
50 Desigual's Diamond Jubilee
    live windows, London.

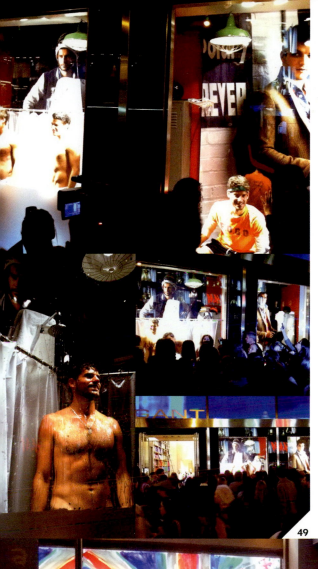

Live windows

The use of live models in retail goes back at least 100 years. Traditionally, we have seen models in department stores wearing merchandise to promote the product to customers and more recently as a means of promotional activity for global brands such as Gant. Top retailers from Galeries Lafayette in Paris and House of Fraser in London to specialist retailers, such as Lush, have all adopted this type of promotion where the outside is brought in and vice versa, generating interest and excitement and attracting passing footfall.

As part of London Fashion Week, H&M created a spectacle by hosting a live fashion shoot with customers and passers-by as the models. Store windows can be more about delivering the live brand experience, giving the customer a memory of a shopping experience to take away, even if they have not purchased anything.

49

50

Interview: Kristofj Von Strass, Beyond Retro

Kristofj Von Strass is Head Visual Merchandiser at vintage clothing brand Beyond Retro. His role involves overseeing all visual merchandising content in the company's three London branches as well as its store in Brighton. He creates the concept of the displays in collaboration with the visual merchandising team and the product department and curates the in-store space for events.

Q What is your brand identity?

A Beyond Retro is quite rock 'n' roll in its approach. We change our displays on a monthly basis and although we work around trends and themes like other retailers will, we don't work with collections. Vintage is evolving in terms of the public's perception so we want to show the full potential of vintage items in a modern look whilst creating a theatrical and memorable story.

Q What is your career background and how did you get into the industry?

A I studied fine art and photography in La Cambre, Brussels. Whilst assisting a fashion photographer in London, I was working as a shop assistant for Beyond Retro. I grabbed every opportunity to help with the displays in store. When the position for Head Visual Merchandiser came up, I applied for it immediately. It helped that I already knew the product, the customers and the brand.

Q How does a new scheme collection development begin?

A It usually starts after Fashion Week. The product department analyses the trends and picks those that are relevant to our customers. I make sure that the themes work with the products that we need to push for the season. I have a folder of everything that I find inspiring (fashion editorials, movies, TV series, exhibitions) and apply it to the scheme.

Q Where do you source your props and generate new ideas?

A We often build our props ourselves using recycled materials. This isn't just down to budget constraints, it's also something we like to have control over. We love recycling old garments for props as it complements the clothes we sell and the brand's philosophy. For our 'Granny Chic' displays we made life-size poodles from recycled jumpers and wool scarves. These worked well against the vintage knits, wool skirts and silk headscarves we wanted to push that season.

Q How do you define your store merchandising against other second-hand, vintage or even charity shops?

A We change our displays every four weeks, which is unusual for a vintage brand. The displays are based around themes and trends, but we also regularly analyse sales to reassess the position of the product in-store. The products positioned on the front displays have got to work together as we want to encourage customers to buy. Vintage is as much a part of people's wardrobes these days as the high street, so we need to understand what our customers want.

Q Is sustainability an important part of your development process?

A Beyond Retro fully supports sustainable fashion. This is clear in every aspect of the business, particularly in our displays as we regularly incorporate recycled items as props and reuse vintage clothing in a dynamic and fun way. We want to encourage customers to shop vintage and use their imagination, rather than dressing head-to-toe in disposable trends.

Interview: Kristofj Von Strass, Beyond Retro

Q Is digital media becoming important in your work?

A It's really important as we're now able to access information quicker than ever before. Sites like Style.com are great as we can watch the shows as soon as they happen. In terms of the brand, digital media and content sharing has really helped improve awareness; we're able to create the atmosphere of the store for those who can't physically make it in.

Q What are the main challenges of creating and delivering a whole installation scheme?

A One challenge is finding the right product to support our concept. Before getting too into an idea, we have to consider product availability and props. We have a small budget but we enjoy pushing ourselves creatively with simple yet effective ideas. The next challenge is to how I communicate my ideas with my team. We work in a tight timeframe, so there's no time to make mistakes and start all over again.

Q How can you measure the impact on sales of your work?

A During and after the theme, we monitor the sales and assess whether it was successful or not. If customers are buying clothes that don't relate to the theme at all, we need to look at how we improve this. As we don't have collections, the aim of visual merchandising at Beyond Retro is always about creating a story that customers will want to buy into. Sales aren't completely dependent on the displays, but if they are high in the appropriate category then we can assume the displays have helped generate this.

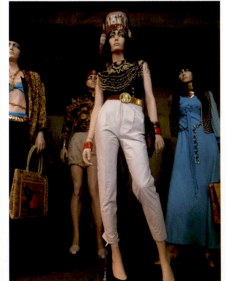

Q **Describe a typical day**

A Most of my days are spent in-store working on the displays, but I'm regularly liaising with each department and with the store managers. There is always a new project to work on and things that staff will need the VM team for, so it's always busy. One day you can be organising an event, the next you're displaying a brand new product that has arrived in-store or even producing a video shoot for the blog. I travel a lot to all the stores as it's very important to keep on top of the visuals and what's in-store.

Q **How long does it take to install a new scheme?**

A We plan at least six months in advance. After we've presented our ideas to the product and press department to confirm delivery times, product and press schedules and key events, I create a preview mood board and the team gets started on sourcing props and creating content.

Q **How do feel when you see a display that you designed dressed to perfection and placed within a store window or space?**

A It's a great feeling. It feels like we've created a scene from a movie! For me, every detail counts: the clothes and the props, the way you place the mannequins, the way you work with the space. You want people to come into your world and interpret the story well.

Interview: Sonya Storm, DZD, London, UK

Sonya Storm is Creative Director at DZD and has worked at the company for 14 years. DZD is the UK's largest supplier of Christmas decorations and seasonal retail display props for the retail market. Sonya oversees the product buying and development within the showroom.

DZD atrium display at Fortnum and Mason, Piccadilly, London.

Q Why did you want to work in designing and producing props/displays?

A I originally began working with larger retailers (department stores) and we often received props and equipment from companies but really never knew where they came from. As I worked up through my career, I began to source props myself and realised that it was something that I had a passion for. As a junior visual merchandiser we were always given instructions on where to place props, mannequins and fixtures and I realised that I would like to be the person who decided that and had more influence in reinforcing the brands' identity.

Q Where does a new scheme collection development begin?

A A new collection might begin with a customer asking for a particular product or it might be something that we have seen in an image somewhere such as a design magazine or tradeshow. We begin by drawing our ideas and sending these out to a range of factories that we want to work with.

Q How do you decide what needs to be produced?

A Occasionally we test potential new products in the showroom and gauge customer interest and response through conversations with them. This might include asking them if the price is at the right level, about the shape of the product, does it need to be more realistic or perhaps iconic; and this happens perhaps twice a year for about 10-15 products at a time.

Q What or who influences the key looks?

A Magazines and fashion in particular are the main influencers of what we do and we keep an eye on the key looks working at least a year in advance.

Interview: Sonya Storm, DZD, London, UK

Q **Is research, development and experimentation an important part of what you decide to produce?**

A Research, development and experimentation is particularly important to us as a company and we work very well in advance. We have to consider who the products are for, test them in ways such as does it need to be electrical, does something need to be in a different colour and so on. We sample all of our products and test them in different sizes and consider who we would produce them for.

Sometimes we have products which we may not particularly like individually, however they may have customer appeal and therefore as part of the process, we need to consider this. We all look and see everything so differently and we understand this and therefore perhaps a client would see something in a different finish for example, and we can arrange to produce it and offer that kind of service. When we manufacture, which we do in the Far East, we lay out products in a room and get a really good overview of the ranges we like and know what would sell and perhaps pick out 25% of the ranges for clients.

Q **What kinds of themes do you produce and what kinds of materials?**

A We produce items for every season, so we have, for example, paper flowers and butterflies for spring, blue sky and cloud fabrics, lollipops for summer, wood papier mâché for autumn - right through to Christmas with trees and baubles. So we produce anything that can be grouped together to support the theme of the season.

Q **How do you think you became so successful in your role?**

A The key things are, I believe, listening to our clients and watching what's happening around us. We build strong relationships with our clients and work very hard to maintain these relationships.

Q What sort of clients do you work with, are they all from retail?

A We work with a whole range of clients. Clients or potential clients are from retail, magazines, film and television and all over the world.

Q Is digital media becoming important in what and how you produce?

A Digital media is becoming more important to us and we use a lot of social media to promote our products rather than us producing digital media ourselves. We also find that what we produce is included in popular media which could be through props being used in films and photo shoots and we often come across our work in magazines or television.

Q What do you love about working in visual merchandising?

A The variety of what we do is incredible. It is a stressful industry and very demanding. Everything needs to be thought through in so much detail. We have to be confident that we have covered and considered everything to ensure that we are delivering exactly what the client wants. No day is a typical day as there is always something new to work on, to develop and deliver.

Q What are the main challenges of creating and delivering a whole display scheme?

A The main challenges are timing and budgets. We manufacture in the Far East and of course there are time constraints on this as we are shipping in our products from such a distance.

THE FUTURE OF VISUAL MERCHANDISING

6

This chapter explores the future of visual merchandising and some of the key innovations in areas such as sustainability, technology and internationalisation.
It looks at the changing demands of the consumer through less traditional platforms such as new retail concepts, virtual and augmented reality, the growth of the market and the further expansion of the visual merchandising industry.

1   Digital display at Mac New York flagship store.

Shopping trends and innovations

Omni retailing, the seamless approach to serving consumers through multi-channels, has brought a new dimension to modern retail. Customers expect to be connected to a brand through a number of different portals, including the physical environment. Digital media now dominates communication with the consumer, but the key in retailing is consistency. The customer expects to be able to see and buy online as well as to try and buy in-store; therefore, the marketing for both a bricks-and-mortar environment and the virtual digital world needs to be consistent in execution to achieve a big impact.

New visual merchandising retail concepts

At store level, retailers are delivering a brand or lifestyle experience in the form of an entertainment, seduction, education and a service. This strategy is designed to tap into the sense of an ideal lifestyle and as such, the retail space needs to be an inspirational environment in which the consumer wants to spend time.

New stores engage with the consumer on many different levels. A department store, for example, may include specific social areas such as a barber shop or cocktail bar; areas for customers to relax and then move on. This strategy delays the customer from leaving the building so they will shop for longer and spend more. Whatever the retail format, whether it is a temporary space, a luxury or value store, the journey experienced needs to be memorable.

Pop-up shops

The temporary pop-up shop concept has taken on various forms from tents, caravans and redundant stores to prime selling spaces in large department stores. The shoe box store by Adidas is an excellent example of creative visual brand positioning. Its strong blue stripe identity and enlarged scale feature produces an unexpected temporary shopping experience for the customer. Online retailers such as eBay are experimenting with bricks-and-mortar channels by launching pop-ups. The ethos of eBay's pop-up shop was to display a selection of products from top-rated sellers that could be purchased on eBay using mobile devices (via smartphone or tablet). Finally, Nike Fuel Station at Boxpark is an exemplary example of how a digital store format can be used to promote product. Housed in the first ever pop-up mall devised from shipping containers, Nike Fuel Station was designed to give customers an innovative digital shopping experience within the physical store. Motion sensitive LED walls, digitised treadmills and interactive touch screens are on display within the box-like store structure.

Visual merchandising trends: where do they come from?

It is essential to keep ahead of new visual merchandising trends and new products. A simple way to do this is to attend the main VM or interior-based trade shows such as EuroShop, Decorex, 100% Design, Mode, Pulse and New Designers, as well as smaller craft fairs of niche groups such as Designers' Block.

Trends are forecast months in advance for each season, with forecast companies imparting inspiration in colour, texture, shapes and new innovations in mannequins, technology and materials. Trend forecasts often include revivals of looks presented in a contemporary package. It is up to the visual merchandiser to decide whether or not to embrace these looks wholeheartedly or interpret the information.

The trickle down, trickle across and bubble up theories explore the ways in which trends emerge, from catwalk to street, and how trends can be adopted across different levels at once.

Trickle down

The trickle down theory relates to the belief that fashion begins at the top of the class structure and spreads downwards at a slow pace to the lower classes. The main fashion influences come from luxury fashion, catwalk shows and exclusive, global trends, driven by differentiation and imitation. The trends are set by the fashion leaders and the consumers who can afford to buy the designs and, thanks to the media, are in a highly visible position to promote the key looks. In terms of visual merchandising this theory can be applied to concept designers working with the likes of Louis Vuitton, Harrods, Bergdorf Goodman and Ralph Lauren, all of whom set the high-end trends through their elite store designs and theatrical and unique visual merchandising.

2 Box Park located in East London is a retail park built from container boxes that form temporary shop shells.

Shopping trends and innovations

3

Trickle across

The trickle-across effect explains how fashion trends move horizontally between social groups to become adopted by the mass market. There is little lag time in adopting the schemes and the speed at which the trends reach mass dissemination is faster compared with trickle down and bubble up. Styles and trends are available in multiple stores at luxury, mid-market and value level. Digital and viral media communications has compounded the trickle-across effect, with retailers able to react to consumer demand quickly and offer interpretations of the trends across different levels at the same time.

However, the trickle-across effect does not always apply. In 2012, American brands Target (a value retailer) and Neiman Marcus (a luxury department store chain) collaborated on a holiday collection. The product was sold by both retailers, but failed to be a success as it did not appeal to the different customers on a mass market level, having stepped too far away from brand image. Neiman Marcus's higher end, 'old money' consumer did not connect with the reputation of Target's brand offer of 'pile it high, sell it cheap'.

4

Trickle up

The trickle-up effect explores the concept of trends and fashions developing from street level. Coco Chanel believed fashion leaders adopted their trends from the lifestyles and needs of women and this supports the theory of fashion trend adoption from lower level to the masses. Street trends often come unpackaged and unlabelled; it is the role of the middle market to turn the trend into something everyone wants and everyone can have, the 'fashionistas' being the next level in adoption. Independent stores and brands that are globally unknown or unrecognised, often in urban centres, encourage the emergence of trends at a grass roots level.

Collaborations

Fashion brands are continuing to collaborate with high profile names, such as Swedish fashion brand H&M, which has worked with world-famous footballer David Beckham and fashion blogger Susie Bubble.
The London department store Liberty often collaborates with brands and designers to use the signature Liberty prints on their products, such as Dr. Martens and Gola. All such collaborations appeal to the consumer market, enabling customers to engage and interact with the brand.

3 Example of a trend interpreted at a high fashion market level.
4 Launch concept digital window.

Shopping trends and innovations

Art installations

Artist collaborations have long been popular in retail design: notable examples include Salvador Dali, Andy Warhol and Vincente Minnelli. The increase in empty retail spaces, thanks to economic recession, present a unique proposition for innovative and thought-provoking installations, to capture and a wider audience. The art of curation borders the visual merchandiser's approach to presenting product within a retail environment.

Individuality and customisation

The shop environment is critical to the memorable experience of the shopper. Converse stores in New York have concentrated the store design to be entirely focused on customer wants and needs. The shopping experience is personal and individual, with in-store services ranging from customer photographic walls, 'make your mark' boot tagging installation and a complete customisation service. Customers can use the latest iPad technology to source product information and availability.

5 Matthew Williamson
collaboration with artist
Kyle Bean.
6 In this House of Fritz Hansen
store, an artist took up residence
in the store window display areas.

WILLIAMSON

5

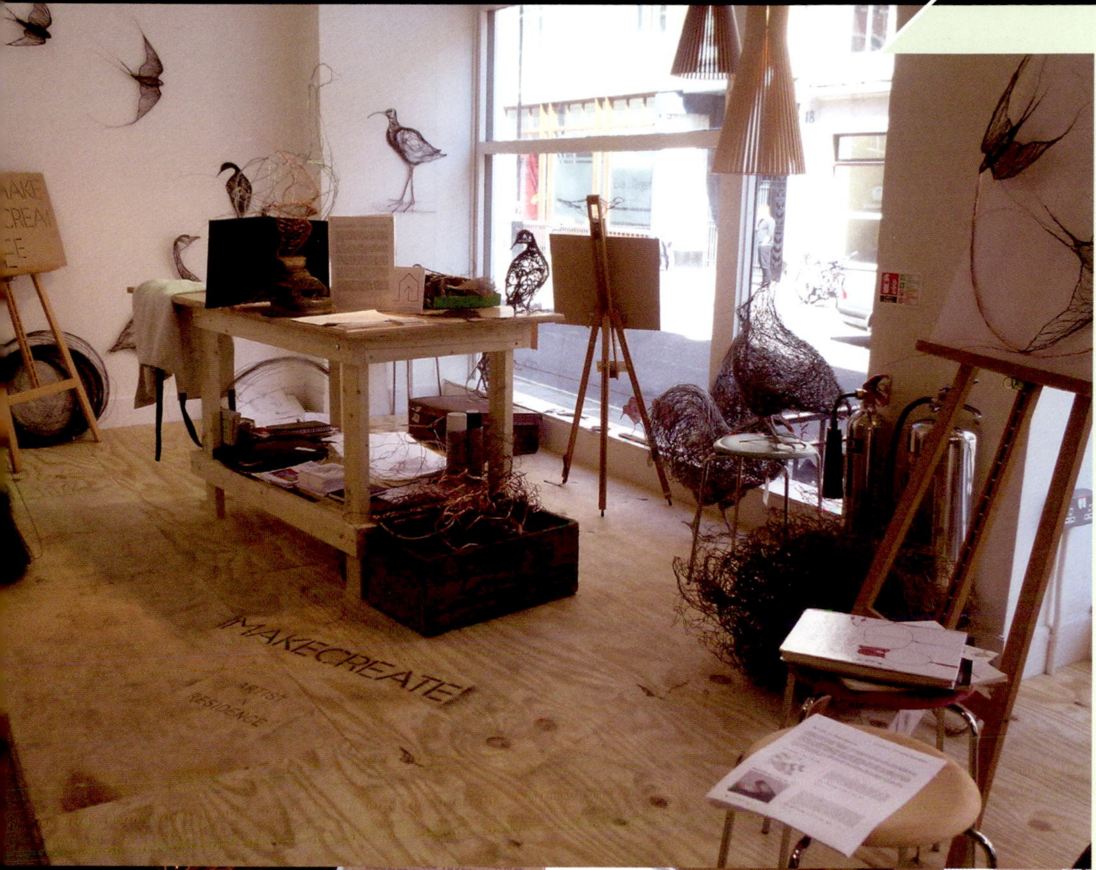

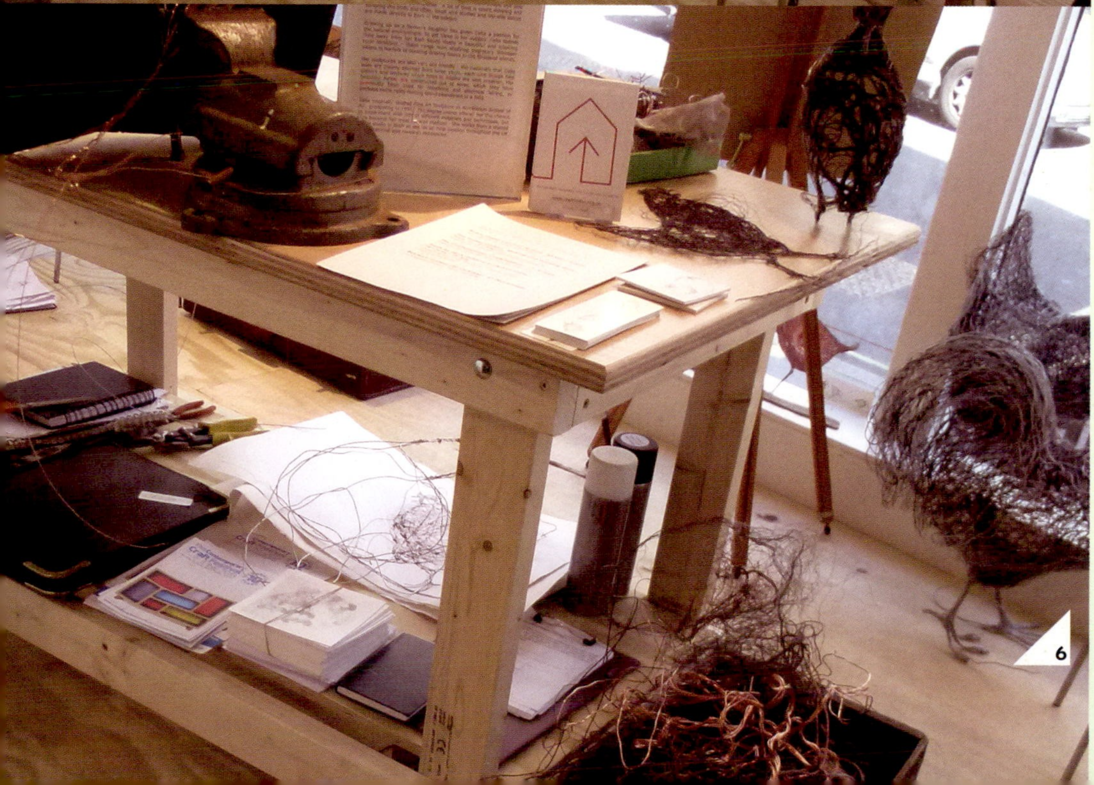

6

Technology and digital visual merchandising

As we move through the 21st century, the technology that makes our shopping experiences faster, smarter, more informed, more interactive and, most importantly, more engaging, is becoming more advanced and sophisticated. Such technology leads us not only through the virtual world but also enhances the experience of the physical one.

This crossover between digital and physical worlds present the visual merchandiser with a challenge to present products in stores. Most recent brand examples prove that the more successful digital installations do not lose touch with the traditional, tactile nature of window schemes. However, some stores have entirely stripped their installations of the 'human touch', which can ultimately disconnect the viewer with the product by keeping it out of reach.

Technology within the commercial space has been widely used across different channels, but it has not yet been fully explored within visual merchandising. Ultimately, technology should simplify the shopping experience and facilitate the sale. Epos systems, scanners and barcodes, for example, all support the function of managing and selling the product, although they do not necessarily enhance the experience of the customer.

Today's modern consumer is technologically savvy, well informed and well connected, posting their opinions via social media and leaving feedback on products. Newspaper, magazine and billboard advertising is no longer enough to maintain their attention. These multi-media savvy customers or DNAs (Digital Natives) are able to switch from one type of media to another with a mere swipe, so it is crucial to a brand's longevity that the customer is engaged.

Interactive digital visual merchandising

Interactive digital visual merchandising can be used to provide information and brand-specific media, combining the benefits of online shopping with a physical retail space. A particularly good example is Perch technology, developed by MIT Media Lab graduates and founders of design and technology firm Potion to provide retailers with tools to increase sales and invigorate the retail environment.

Practical uses can include:

×   Product descriptions and any technical specifications that may appeal to a customer
×   Online reviews and ratings by customers who have previously bought a particular product, which contributes to the authenticity and reliability of the brand
×   Social media connections and feeds to encourage longer interaction
×   Visual imagery from photo shoots that may tie in with an existing brand campaign, which can be supported with sound effects and animation
×   Lighting effects used to create exciting focal points within a retail space
×   Suggestions of additional potential sales purchases
×   Gesture tracking that follows customer movements within the projected space
×   Product identification
×   Interaction tracking that monitors frequency and type of customer interaction, such as products of interest

Virtual reality

Virtual reality is the digital means of simulating a physical presence. Virtual reality scenarios can be traced back to the panoramas of the Victorian era, albeit in low technical specifications, so the concept of walking through a hyper-realistic, three-dimensional space is by no means a new one. The technology is mainly used in visual merchandising to illustrate digital walks through a simulated computer-generated space.

Simulated reality

Simulated reality is similar to virtual reality although it further blurs the boundaries of what is real; these digitally produced environments can be indistinguishable from reality.

Augmented reality

Augmented reality in visual merchandising is currently used as an interactive tool. It enables a customer to 'try on' a product without actually having to undress in a fitting room. Virtual mirrors are a great example of augmented reality (see page 166.)

Technology and digital visual merchandising

Augmented virtuality

Augmented virtuality within commercial spaces, while not yet widely used, is the integration of a virtual spaces with real objects such as fixtures, mannequins and so on. This presents opportunities for retailers to have virtual stores with real products placed within them.

Avatars

Avatars are simulated graphic images of a real person or a personality connected to the online user. They are not widely used in retailing however, and are generally used in computer generated gaming rather than commercial spaces.

Mediated reality

Retailers are increasingly using mediated reality in smartphone apps to engage with customers. It involves visually enhancing an actual environment with computer-generated images: StreetFinder is probably the best current example of this technology.

Multi-modal input

Probably the best-known application of multi-modal input is the combination of a computer keypad or keyboard and mouse along with speech recognition, which increases usability and accessibility for customers, especially those with visual or hearing impairments.

Virtual continuum

Virtual continuum is more commonly known as mixed reality, which encompasses augmented reality, augmented virtuality and virtual reality. While there is little research currently as to its potential use in visual merchandising, applications could include product placement, advertising opportunities or simply brand awareness.

Life-like experiences

Life-like experiences refer to anything which through immersive technology simulates real life as it is or as it may be. Examples currently in use include driving test technology where participants can learn to drive a vehicle without being on the road itself.

Kinetic technology wall

Digital walls are designed as an architectural element.

Digital floors and stairs

Louis Vuitton's flagship store in London features an illuminated, animated staircase that displays moving imagery. Some shopping malls, such as those in Dubai, for example, also contain digital floors that double up as catwalks when not being used as part of the main thoroughfare.

Shopping apps

Harrods has an in-store shopping app (application) to help customers navigate through the vast offering of luxury merchandise. Apps are easily downloaded from a scanned image and enable customers to destination shop by directing them to the relevant department. Apps are also an ideal solution for foreign visitors, offering navigation and communication in any selected language.

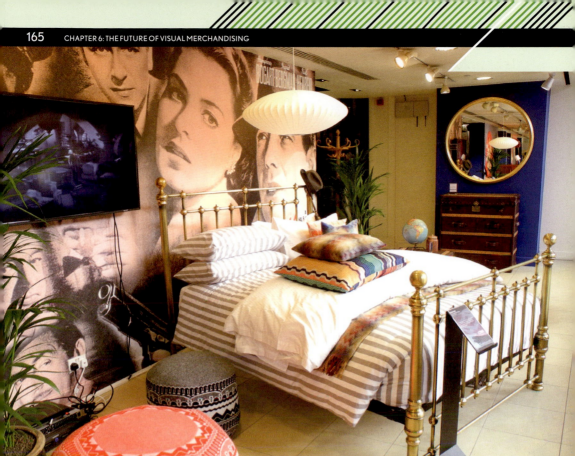

7

Digital sound

With digital sound, any solid surface can become the speaker. Loud speaker retail windows and interactive systems can be used to present digital content such as photographs, videos, product details, social media and user reviews all within one digital 'visual'. UK-based company Feonic developed a technology called 'invisible audio', which is designed to deliver high-quality audio output by attaching speakers to a resonant material such as glass, wood, plasterboard or metal.

Feonic collaborated with Heal's on its interactive window campaign, 'Whispering windows'. The installation featured iconic film footage from *Gone with the Wind*, *Casablanca* and an episode of *Tom and Jerry*. Audio technology was used to convert the windows into speakers by evenly distributing sound across the entire window surface, which enabled customers to hear the film track both inside and outside the store.

7   Heals, London,
    Whispering window.

Technology and digital visual merchandising

Visual broadcasting systems

Communicating with customers via digital screens is an effective approach for visual merchandisers: it enables marketing opportunities that are active and dynamic instead of static. The content needs to be changed frequently, which adds to the retailer's annual budget, in some cases quite significantly, but the advantages are that the content can be shared between multiple stores.

Virtual mirrors

Virtual or 'magic' mirrors are a form of augmented technology used by retailers the world over. A digital screen enables the customer to search a collection through intuitive hand gestures and virtually try on the products. A computer identifies the size and gender of the customer while matching their body shape with an item of clothing. An image of the customer wearing the product can then be viewed on screen. Such technology offers the time-poor customer a quick and easy solution. The virtual mirrors also enable a brand to communicate its latest campaign and engage with passing footfall. One limitation is that the image appears quite flat and two-dimensional; however, as the product develops with greater sophistication, a three-dimensional view could soon be available.

8

Immersive 360-degree projection

So far immersive 360-degree projection has primarily been used in the cultural and performing arts, but companies such as UK-based Igloo Vision have been commercialising the technology and transporting audiences to an imaginary destination or virtual environment.
The technology has been used for corporate events, military applications, cultural events, festivals and the emergency services, and there is definite potential for retail applications.

Digital hangers

Digital hangers contain a chip that activates a screen when a customer pulls the item from the rail; this screen presents other garments that could be worn with it.
Such technology brings a whole new meaning to outfit building in visual merchandising. Digital hangers can also be used to gauge popularity of a product, such as the amount of times a product is liked on Facebook, for example.

8 Digital projection by Digital Igloo.

Technology and digital visual merchandising

Digital mannequins

Digital mannequins help to sell product without taking up valuable selling space. The technology involves the projection of images, with regular garment changes to show different combinations available. Italian-based mannequin company Almax has created a digital-based project 'Eyesee Mannequin'. A camera with analytical software is installed in the head of a mannequin to track consumer behaviour and provide data such as the number of people passing a window at specific times of the day.

9   Digital window at Saks, image taken in New York.
10   Digital window display at Topshop during London Fashion Week.

10

Sustainability

In a globally dominated fashion retail industry the consideration for sustainability in visual merchandising could and should be moving a lot faster. Visual merchandising by its very nature is dynamic, idiosyncratic, ephemeral; it promotes innovation and inspiration and creates aspiration. It can also be disorderly and uncontrolled and, if used incorrectly, pointless or worse still, damaging to the brand. In our contemporary society it is important that the brand combines innovation in visual merchandising with concern for the environment. This is not simply a case of creating sustainable visual merchandising in a sustainable market, it has to be adopted at a universal level, in the overall retail design vision rather than in isolation.

Modern consumer culture has solved a lot of social problems by enabling better lifestyles but this has come at an environmental price. Visual merchandising design has a unique role in providing solutions that could address these issues. It is not enough for a brand to simply design a 'green theme' or 'eco window', or to create props from old tyres and recycled paper; sustainability starts at a grass roots level. Multiple resources are wasted in the visual merchandising process. Modern consumers are increasingly scrutinising visual merchandising and retail design in terms of environmental impact and sustainability. A sustainable growth strategy should begin at the visual merchandising design stage and include the store build and architecture as well as the micro-visual merchandising elements such as fixtures, mannequins and props.

11

Sustainable visual merchandising checklist

×   Propose to use reusable, reclaimed, recyclable or eco materials at design stage
×   Themes adopted for window displays can support the activities related to sustainability, ethical fashion or social/corporate responsibility
×   Investigate ethical origins of display materials and mannequins, with regard to where they are sourced and how they are produced, ensuring that suppliers comply with sustainable processes
×   Examine the production of display materials in terms of workers and labour rights.
×   Consider the country of origin in terms of delivery and logistics; how far does your visual merchandising scheme travel from manufacture before it reaches the store destination?
×   Review lighting usage and store energy levels
×   Identify consumption levels and wastage within visual merchandising schemes
×   Use sustainability within the visual merchandising marketing and branding campaign as part of a larger corporate responsibility

Living nature in store design

Customers are more likely to spend time in environments with natural light or natural features – it is human instinct. Plants such as moss can be used to soundproof certain areas and even keep areas of buildings warm. Using natural elements such as vegetated walls in store design can serve more than an aesthetic purpose: plants also provide oxygen, reduce sound levels and even balance the air temperature. Research indicates that plants or vegetation can control humidity and improve air quality, especially in air-locked environments such as stores within shopping malls.

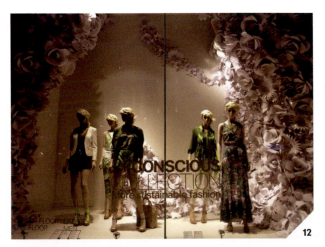

11 Harvey Nichols recycled furniture scheme.
12 H&M Conscious Collection, sustainable fashion, London.

Sustainability

Reclaim, recycle and reform

Using found objects in visual merchandising is a sustainable approach; the world is full of redundant objects that could be reused in a creative manner. Nike has launched Nike Reuse-A-Shoe campaign, which recycles sports shoes into running tracks, basketball courts and new Nike products.

Reformation or upcycling is the customisation of vintage items for a new purpose and many independent fashion designers have taken this approach with their products. American brand Anthropologie upcycles objects in its creative visual displays; items such as teabags, paper cups, plastic bottles and old household objects become the basis of new, inspiring visual merchandising – so much so that the customer almost wouldn't recognise their original purpose.

13

Retail activists

Responsible recycling campaigns encourage customers to shop in a sustainable way, to think about the items they are replacing by bringing old products back to trade in. British brand Marks & Spencer launched a 'Shwopping' initiative that aimed to resell donated old M&S garments to raise money for charity and to keep items out of landfill. All M&S clothing stores now accept unwanted clothing of any brand, all year round, which aims to create a more sustainable 'buy one, give one' culture on the UK high street. M&S also collaborated with London College of Fashion's Centre For Sustainable Fashion to open Schwop Lab, the UK's first sustainable fashion lab, in the heart of East London.

13 Marks & Spencer, Shwopping with Joanna Lumley, London.

Sustainable mannequins

From the mid-20th century onwards, mannequins have been made using synthetic materials such as fibreglass, which cannot be recycled. However, there are a number of mannequin companies that operate in a more sustainable way. Award-winning La Rosa Mannequins is the only company in the world that manufactures mannequins in full respect of the environment and workers' rights. Almax has launched a 'Greener Window' initiative, whereby clients can have their old mannequins taken away free of charge, irrespective of their condition, for every mannequin purchased. And in 2009, Cofrad developed a 100% vegetable fibreglass manufacturing process; a sustainable method of production. As well as manufacturing mannequins, Cofrad also has a renovation and resale network for used mannequins. Extending the life of existing products is one more step towards sustainability.

14 Cheshire Oaks Store is a sustainable learning store (SLS), which is part of the M&S 'Plan A' commitment to sustainable building practices. This carbon efficient, biodiverse and materially innovative store has achieved a BREEAM excellent rating (the world's foremost environmental assessment). The building features a timber and recycled aluminium roof, Hemclad walls and a vegetated living wall. No waste is sent to landfill and 25% of the store's water is supplied via rainwater harvesting. Investments in customer travel routes to and from the store have been included in the sustainable construction plan, as has the preservation of local trees, plant life and wildlife.

14

Internationalisation

Approaches to visual styling and
merchandising should be adapted by
any fashion brand launching into new
countries or markets. The interpretation
of looks, preferences in the ways
garments are worn and even the ways
in which people shop, are different
around the world. The key to maintaining
strength and image of a brand or visual
profile while reaching out to a global
audience is by tapping into the local
mindset, observing and listening to
cultural/social differences and working
with local people.

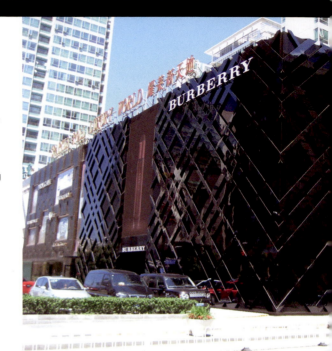

Visual guidelines and directives are imperative to achieve the right visual merchandising standards for a brand anywhere in the world. One way in which companies launch a fashion brand in a different country is by working with a franchise partner, which offers rewards in local knowledge and understanding.

The Middle East

In Dubai a shopping culture is embedded in people's everyday lives. Customers shop day and night in the world famous mega malls, which have become all-inclusive leisure destinations where you can not only shop but can also ski, watch a movie, take a boat trip, visit an aquarium, ice skate, watch fireworks and spend the night. Dubai Mall opened in 2008 with over 1,200 retail outlets. A traditional souk sits alongside global designer brands such as Fendi, Dior, Gucci and Ralph Lauren.

Trading laws and regulations in the Middle East are quite different from anywhere else in the world. Restrictions on promotional and sale merchandise mean that many Western brands are required to trade within local licensing regulations, which vary according to state. Sale times do not always run in line with other countries, which can make the commercial and visual strategy a more complex process.

In Saudi Arabia stores have strict regulations on showing the human figure. Point of sale can show merchandise but not include image representation of the body. Visual merchandisers working for fashion brands in Saudi Arabia have the added challenge of presenting merchandise without the use of mannequins or graphics; schemes must be converted to fit the local market in order not to break local trading laws or cause offence to customers.

Cultural occasions

In some countries, such as the Philippines, Christmas is a year-round celebration. Customers here favour lavish visual merchandising and heavily decorated interiors. Being aware of such cultural preferences enables the visual merchandiser to design interior and window schemes that reflect the customer mindset and deliver to expectation. Christmas in the United States is also big business, with people travelling worldwide to view the spectacular window installations that entertain the passing footfall, particularly in cities such as New York and Chicago.

Second tier markets

Fashion brands in particular are beginning to expand into 'second tier' markets rather than the already acquired big cities of emerging market places. Smaller towns or cities, which are located away from the biggest or most notorious development sites, are being targeted as new locations for expansion.

15 Major store franchises in China, France and Dubai.

Interview: Bryan Meszaros, OpenEye

Bryan Meszaros is director of OpenEye, a digital media consultancy with a focus on designing strategic digital in-store experiences.

Q How did you get into the industry?

A I personally have been involved with digital media since university, graduating with a degree in communication arts. When I started in this industry (digital out-of-home) there was more of an emphasis on the technology than the design side. We started to hear our clients ask for more creative methods to use visual technology beyond 'atmospheric branding' or to fill a void in the store. It was at that point we became interested in understanding how technology could be treated as a design element within the store.

Our emphasis grew towards consumer engagement but we realised what was displayed on the screen was only part of the solution. How technology appeared in the environment would ultimately determine its success.

Q Can you describe how you work within retail?

A We help retailers better understand how they can connect with their customers through the usual of visual and interactive technology. We advise them on how they can harness the latest trends to create in-store experiences that add value to the customer.

Q   **Where does technology fit into visual merchandising?**

A   Every brand is trying to tell a story and create a visual relationship with their customer, which hopefully leads to a transaction of some sort. Whether it's a mobile interaction or a touch display, there is that moment in which the consumer expects to interact with the experience. I think it comes down to using visual technology to bring the experiences/stories to life. Technology helps to better engage the consumer and bring them into the experience.

MAC initially integrated a large format digital display within its New York flagship store in SoHo. It is positioned towards the front of the store, close enough to the window to draw attention from the sidewalk but also angled to greet customers. MAC uses it as more of a campaign tool, bringing to life its dramatic product photos. Since New York it has gone on to install the same type of display at the Paris and Waikiki stores. The display was designed by Nanolumens.

Gilly Hicks took an interesting approach by digitising its entire storefront. It's mostly atmospheric but still draws the attention of the customer. Not all the stores have this treatment but the shop within the Westfield Stratford is a good example.

Interview: Bryan Meszaros, OpenEye

Q **How do you decide on what new technology should be integrated?**

A We look at the consumer. Who are they and what are their expectations of the brand? How do they currently interact with the brand, for example, mobile phone, iPad applications, social media. Once we build a consumer profile we can than understand what technology elements will complement their existing behaviours.

Q **How do you decide what needs to be produced?**

A When we work with a client we start by understanding what challenges they are facing in-store. Is it a lack of customer communication, decrease in brand equity, lack of sales? From that point we begin to develop a solution for the client.

Q **How is digital media becoming important and how are you reacting to this?**

A The simplest answer is that consumers expect to see and interact with technology in the store. So for us it's more about helping our clients better understand what trends are emerging and how can they utilise them to meet the growing demand of their customers.

Q What are the main challenges of creating and delivering technology to support a retail display scheme?

A Technology has a lot of hidden challenges that many brand do not think of. For example:
× Connectivity – most brands don't realise that connectivity is necessary to support and deliver information to all channels whether it be mobile, digital signage or intercity.
× Technical support – as with technology in your house, someone needs to fix it!

Q Describe a typical day

A I love the word typical, do people have typical days? Mine starts at about 8am and if I'm lucky will end around midnight! A typical day has us doing a headline search in the morning (what's new in the retail world) followed by a mid-morning sketch session and the afternoon is reserved for team meetings and client brainstorming sessions.

Q What do you love about working in visual merchandising?

A I love the storytelling aspect of visual merchandising. I enjoy being able to communicate with a consumer in a method that is not directly advertising. It's being able to use creativity and technology, in a subtle manner, to explain why they should be interested in this brand/product.

Activities

The following activities are intended as a guide to get
you started. They all involve observing existing schemes
and displays in the stores you visit. But you should also
try to put your own ideas into practice - how might
you have done something differently? Do you think the
schemes work? How much do you think they might have
cost? Draw, sketch, visualise your own ideas and think
about how they might work.

Brand awareness

Part 1

Think about the last store you visited that you
have never shopped in before.

× Why did you decide to go there?
× Were you responding to a specific advertising
campaign?
× What did you see when you walked in?
× Did the store's exterior send you any messages?
× Was the storefront appealing? Was it informative?
× When you entered, was the level of lighting pleasant?
× Do you remember any particular scent or sounds?
× Was it easy to tell to identify the brand?
× On your visit what was the impression of
the store?

Part 2

Take note of the following window installation
factors:

× Is the installation visually attractive? What does it
communicate about the brand/products?
× Viewing point/direction of the window
× How many windows are there?
× What level is the window at?
× How do/does the window(s) work with the
architecture of the store?
× Signage and brand/store logo: is it visible?

Windows analysis

Part 1:

Visit a variety of retailers and identify the trends for a particular season:

Colour

Footwear

Accessories

Materials

New products

Consider how these trends are translated into window schemes. Which products are new for this year? Using a matrix, identify which retailers you have looked at and photographed, and list the products, colours, materials.

For example:

Part 2:

Record images and schemes regularly by observing what type of display dynamics have been exercised in the windows. Use the information throughout this chapter to note:

× Use of colour
× Use of shape and form
× Use of materials:
× Use of lighting:

Retailer	Date and Image	Colour trend	Materials	Product	Fashion / Food /
Name	Image and date here				
Name	Image and date here				
Name	Image and date here				
Name	Image and date here				
Name	Image and date here				
Name	Image and date here				
Name	Image and date here				

Activities

Visual merchandising store audit

Select at least two comparative stores and conduct the following audit:

Store name

Store location

Building to the left of store

Building to the right of store

Building opposite

Date of visit

Time of visit

Competitors

Exterior and windows
- × Overall building – architecture/period
- × Fascia/shop front
- × Corporate identity
- × Entrances/exits
- × What is the first thing you notice in the windows?
- × What are the main focal points in the window?
- × What dressing style is used?
- × What is the main message to the viewer?
- × What is the overall window theme/scheme?
- × What is the concept?
- × How is the window communicating the brand identity?
- × How is the product presented?
- × Mannequins – type, poses, composition
- × Describe props
- × Describe product
- × Lighting (directional, atmospheric, and so on)
- × Standards
- × Graphics/POS

Store layout
- × Number of floors and entrances
- × Placement of product categories on different floors
- × How is the product segmented into departments/areas?
- × What are the product adjacencies?
- × Customer flow through escalators, entrances, stairs, lifts
- × Customer navigation
- × Focal points
- × Pause points
- × Customer circulation / the 'journey'
- × Product density
- × Till points
- × Service areas
- × Customer service / information points
- × Fitting rooms
- × Perimeter walls

Elements of design
- × Overall ambience
- × Wall treatments
- × Floor treatments
- × Ceiling treatments
- × Materials used in store design
- × Colour
- × Texture
- × Trends
- × Lighting
- × Temperature
- × Music
- × Digital engagement
- × Interior signage
- × Visual communications

Equipment and display materials
× Main fixture types
× Materials used in fixtures and furniture
× Tables
× Mannequins
× Props and display aids
× Hanging (lateral and side facing merchandise)
× Shelving (folded merchandise)
× Freestanding fixtures
× Hangers
× Display density of product
× Display coordination
× Display signage at fixture level

Product
× How is the merchandise presented, e.g. colour blocked, tops over bottoms?
× Brands and own brands
× Type of product categories available
× Core product
× Fashion product
× Fashion collections
× Product information communicated
× Brand messages
× Pricing strategy
× Promotions
× Out-posting
× Impulse merchandising
× Any key visual looks created with product

Graphics and POS
× How is price communicated in-store?
× Features and benefits of product
× What type of language was used in-store to talk to the customer?
× Tone of voice when communicating
× How is point of sale implemented?
× Store guides and navigation
× Point-of-sale material
× Journey graphics
× Is the external marketing message consistent in-store?

Customers
× Age group
× Demographic of customer
× Any particular shopping groups; are customers shopping alone or with others?
× From observations how much time on average do customers spend in store?
× Customer behaviour
× What would tempt you to buy in the store?
× Who is the target customer?
× Do the customers look or dress like they belong to the brand?

Customer experience
× How do the customers navigate through the store?
× Did the displays follow on in-store from the windows?
× Was the brand message consistent throughout the store?
× Use five key words to summarise your observations from the store visit
× What five recommendations would you suggest to the management team as they plan their layout and displays for next season?
× What was your final opinion of the store?

Include any photos or visual references to support your findings.

Activities

Fixtures

Keep a record of the wide variety of
merchandise fixtures that are available on
the high street, in the form of a visual audit.
You must first ask the retailer for permission
to photograph a store interior. Use the
following table as a guide.

Name of brand	Type of retail	Location fixture types	Additional information/images

Visual research

Part 1
Visit an exhibition of your choice, recording the following in your sketch book:
× What inspired you most about this exhibition?
× What techniques, styles, colours, fabrics or influences have you adopted from the exhibition for your visual research?

Follow up your research on one of the areas or artists you have found interesting, in an aspect that is relevant to a current design project, and explain how you will apply what you have learnt to your design project.

Explore existing ideas and turn them upside down to create a different meaning and approach to your work.

Part 2
Select one word and thoroughly investigate it through mind mapping and means of visualisation. Compare and discuss difference in interpretation and meaning with other students. What are the connotations and denotations of the word and how have these been recorded? Note the variations in imagery and illustration that have been explored. What common themes and associations are emerging? Are there any unusual links? Explore all creative possibilities to gain new perspectives on the given subject.

Resources

Industry associations and contacts

Associations

ARE – Association for Retail Environments
www.retailenvironments.org
BREEAM – Standard for best practice in
sustainable building design www.bream.org
British Display Society
www.britishdisplaysociety.co.uk
FSC – Forest Stewardship Council
www.ic.fsc.org
ISO – International Organization for
Standardisation www.iso.org
PAVE – The Planning & Visual Education
Partnership www.paveinfo.org
VM & Display Directory
www.vmanddisplay.com
VMM – European Visual Marketing
Merchandising Association www.vmm.eu

Research and journals

A1 Lighting www.a1lightingmagazine.com
A1 Retail www.a1retailmagazine.com
DDI Online www.ddionline.com
Dezeen Magazine www.dezeen.com
Drapers Record www.drapersonline.com
Emerald Insight www.emeraldinsight.com
Mintel www.mintel.com
Retail Design & Technology Magazine
www.rdtmagazine.co.uk
Retail Environments
www.retailenvironments-digital.org
Retail Focus Magazine www.retail-focus.co.uk
Retail Week www.retail-week.com
Retail Week Interiors www.retail-week.com
Style Guide Magazine www.style-guide.biz
VMSD Magazine www.vmsd.com
W.G.S.N www.wgsn.com

Visual merchandising shows and exhibitions

ARE (Association for Retail Environments) –
Retail Design Collective, New York, USA
www.retaildesigncollective.com
Euroshop – Dusseldorf, Germany
www.euroshop-tradefair.com
Global Shop – USA www.globalshop.org
IDW – Visual Merchandising and Display Show
London, UK www.vmanddisplay.com

Related design, trend and interiors shows

100% Design, UK
www.100percentdesign.co.uk
Bread & Butter, Berlin, Germany
www.breadandbutter.com
Decorex, London, UK www.decorex.com
Interiors LDN, London, UK
www.interiorsuk.com
Maison Objet, Paris, France
www.maison-objet.com
Pulse, London, UK www.pulse-london.com
Surface Design show – London, UK
www.surfacedesignshow.com
Tent London, UK www.tentlondon.co.uk
Top Drawer, UK www.topdrawer.co.uk

Suppliers to the visual merchandising industry

Mannequin suppliers

ABC Manichini
www.abcitalia.com
Almax
www.almax-italy.com
Bonavari
www.bonaveri.com
Cofrad Mannequins
www.cofrad.com
Hansboot Mannequins
www.hansboodtmannequins.com
La Rosa
www.larosaitaly.com
Proportion>London
www.proportionlondon.com
Rootstein
www.rootstein.com
Stockman
www.siegel-stockman.com
Universal Display
www.universaldisplay.co.uk

Visual merchandising design specialists

Barthelmess
www.barthelmess.com
Blacks Visual Merchandising
www.blacks-vm.com
Chameleon Visual
www.chameleonvisual.co.uk
Concorde Graphics
www.concordegraphics.com
D1 Design and Creative
www.displayone.co.uk
DZD
www.dzd.co.uk
Elemental Design
www.elemental.co.uk
Harlequin Design
www.harlequin-design.com
Matt Wingfield
www.mattwingfieldstudio.com
Minki Balinki
www.minkibalinki.com
PLANarama
www.planarama.com
Prop Studios
www.propsstudios.co.uk
Rare Basic
www.rarebasic.co.uk
Replica
www.replica.co.uk
SFD – Shop Fittings Direct
www.sfd.co.uk

Glossary

ATV
Average transaction value. This is the average spend of a customer, calculated by dividing the number of transactions by amount of money received.

Base plate
Used to hold a mannequin upright. Generally made of glass or steel, these are circular or square in shape.

Bottom forms or trunks
Lower half of a mannequin, usually used for swimwear, lingerie or underwear.

Bust form/torso
A mannequin cut off at the waist, thighs or neck. Tailored bust forms are produced in fabric, making it easier to dress and present product thanks to the tactile nature.

Closed merchandising
Presentation of high end or valuable products in locked cabinets.

Colour blocking
presentation of merchandise using colour groups, sequences and combinations according to colour wheel theories/principles.

Core range
Products that are always in stock and that never change.

Customer journey
The experience a client has with a brand.

Design process
The journey and order of development from research through to design development and final piece.

Dual site/dual positioning
Merchandising products in more than one place. Especially relevant when a product can be sold with more than one item to enhance link sales and outfit building.

Fascia
External front of a store that surrounds the window spaces and usually contains the brand name and logo.

Focal point
The point to which the eye is automatically drawn. Multiple focal points can exist in stores and windows.

Footfall
The amount of people walking through the store or an area of the store.

Hot spot
Area in a store that every customer sees or passes by, has high footfall and exposure.

Impulse merchandising
Unplanned purchases. Retailers merchandise low-value items such as socks, lip balm and umbrellas within the queuing area or next to higher priced items.

JTS
Journey to sale (also known as point of sale – see POS). Consists of printed materials within the commercial environment, visuals, directional signage, promotional signage, product descriptors as well as advertising outside of the space, all of which support the customer journey.

Limited editions
Designed to create urgency, great for increasing the average transaction value (ATV).

Link sales
Placement of one product next to another to create a spark or encourage the customer to buy more (for example, cleanser with an exfoliator, TV and DVD player).

Logical adjacencies
Similar to link sales but the layout follows a logical sequence in the way a customer would use the product, for example bras followed by knickers, shirts followed by ties and so on.

Logo
Recognisable artwork to represent a distinct image or brand name.

Merchandising strategy
The plan for product positioning within the retail store space. It is based upon getting the right product in the right place at the right time.

Open merchandising
Fashion product that is laid out to be touched, picked up and tried on by the customer.

POS
Point of sale. Less accurate description for journey to sale – see JTS.

Price blocking
Merchandising products with the same price point together.

Promotional lines
Limited editions, seasonal ranges or buy it now pieces that are merchandised differently to stand out from a brand's core range (but should also be consistent with a core range).

Pyramid format
Pyramid-shaped design format used in product presentation. This format is also used as a focal point central to an installation.

Research
Inspirational sources used to produce inspiration that leads towards design development. Primary research is original content sourced by the researcher; secondary research is the analysis of images or ideas that come from existing sources.

Rule of three or five
Merchandising theory based on the principle that items look better in groups of three or five (as opposed to even numbers). Mannequins are sometimes presented in this arrangement.

Seasonal merchandising
Merchandising that reflects the time of year, such as Christmas, Easter, Valentine's Day and so on.

Sensory store environment
Designing an environment to appeal to customers' senses.

Shopping flow
The direction customers take on entering a store. The flow can be manipulated by walkways and circulation paths or product placement.

Spigot
Metal rod inserted into the leg or foot of a mannequin to connect it to the base plate.

Tailored bust forms
Traditional cloth-covered tailor's mannequins without heads. Usually featuring a central pole to adjust the height, these forms are easy to pin onto and tailor product.

Upselling
The effective use of selling skills and product knowledge to encourage customers to buy more, for example the customer enters the store for a shirt and leaves with a shirt and matching tie.

Visual merchandising
Putting the art and design into retail and commercial environments. Visual merchandising is used to communicate how to use or wear a product or service and enables the retailer to combine a range of components to entice the customer to purchase more.

Index

Acknowledgements and picture credits

With special thanks:

Maxine Groucott
Emma Davidge
Edward Stammers
Andi Grant
Paul Brooks
Patrick Minkley
Bryan Meszaros
Kristofj Von Strass
Sonya Storm
Kevin Arpino
Dillys Williams
Daniel Himsworth
Matt Wingfield
Laurent Paoli
Danny Letton
Deborah Millington
Moe Krimat
Andrew Brown
Tanya Reynolds
Julianne Lavery
Gemma Emslie
Edward Fitzgerald
Tess Richardson
Melvin Vincent

Picture credits:

All reasonable attempts have been made
to trace, clear and credit the copyright
holders of the images reproduced in
this book. However, if any credits have
been inadvertently omitted, the publisher will
endeavour to incorporate amendments
in future editions.

Almax
ABC Manichini
Barthelmess
Ben Sherman (photography: Karl Donovan)
Beyond Retro
Blacks Visual Merchandising

Chameleon Visual
Cofrad Mannequins
D1 Design & Creative
DZD
Elemental Design
Feonic
Gant
Hackett
Harlequin Design (London) Ltd
Harrods
Heals
House of Fritz Hansen
Igloo Vision
La Rosa Mannequins
Liberty London
MAC (via Nanolumens)
Maison Martin Margiela
Marks & Spencer
Matches Fashion
Alexander McQueen
Minki Balinki
Openeye
Perch Technology
Proportion>London
Rare Basic (Nick Haigh)
Rootstien
SFD
Splash
Universal Display

Lara Balbaligo
Chi Ho Lai
Magdalena Choluj
Ena Hung
Jin Young Bae
Louise Kidger
Qian Koh
Natalia Misiun
Sasha Molyneux